The 500 Hidden Secrets of

BERLIN

INTRODUCTION

This is a guide for readers who want to discover the heart and soul of Berlin. The 500 addresses and facts you'll find here have been carefully selected by the author, Nathalie Dewalhens, who lost her heart to the city in 2012.

This guide doesn't tell you everything there is to see; there are already plenty of books and websites that cover the familiar tourist places. The aim here is to take the reader to unexpected places, like a small Turkish restaurant near a canal, or a photo gallery in a hidden courtyard. The selection is highly personal, however this does not mean that the addresses in this book are all the author's personal favourites. Instead, she has tried to present as many of Berlin's different sides as possible. There's effervescent, hip Berlin with all its vegan-and-gluten-free-hipster coffee bars and men with beards; there's luscious, green Berlin with its unique parks and lakes; and there's beautiful (former) West-Berlin, as magnificent and grand as Paris. The author also pays attention to Berlin's bustling and wild nightlife.

The author hopes that with this book tucked in your pocket, you'll be set to go out and make your own discoveries. New designers and artists come to the city every day and open shops there; there are always new museums and galleries popping up. The city is always moving. In fact it's still being built up every day – the many cranes in the streets are there to prove it. If you keep this book in your hands and your eyes and mind open, you'll soon understand why Berlin is one of the most interesting and one of the most loved cities in Europe.

HOW TO
USE THIS BOOK?

This guide lists 500 things you need to know about Berlin in 100 different categories. Most of these are places to visit, with practical information to help you find your way. Others are bits of information that help you get to know the city and its habitants. The aim of this guide is to inspire, not to cover the city from A to Z.

The places listed in the guide are given an address, including a district (for example Friedrichshain or Mitte), and a number. The district and number allow you to find the locations on the maps at the beginning of the book. Look for the map of the corresponding district, and then look for the number. A word of caution however: these maps are not detailed enough to allow you to locate specific locations in the city. A detailed map can be obtained from any tourist information centre or from most good hotels. Or the addresses can be located on a smartphone.

Please also bear in mind that cities change all the time. The chef who hits a high note one day may be uninspiring on the day you happen to visit. The hotel ecstatically reviewed in this book might suddenly go down-hill under a new manager. This is obviously a highly personal selection. You might not always agree with it. If you want to leave a comment, recommend a bar or reveal your favourite secret place, please visit the website *the500hiddensecrets.com* – you'll also find free tips and the latest news about the series there – or follow *@500hiddensecrets* on Instagram and leave a comment.

THE AUTHOR

After having lived in Belgium, Corsica and the South of France, Nathalie Dewalhens ended up in Berlin in 2012. She quickly fell in love with the city, and immediately considered it home. In 2022, her nomadic lifestyle led her to Andalusia, but just like Marlène Dietrich sang in 1954: *Ich hab' noch einen Koffer in Berlin* (I still have a suitcase in Berlin). And she always will.

Nathalie loves exploring Berlin by bike. Sometimes she stops at a friendly bar to work while sipping a soy cappuccino; sometimes she's out and about, meeting people and organising poetry events, and sometimes she just drives to one of the city's many parks, to have an ice cream or a beer with friends. Her favourite spots are often located in former no man's land, where the Wall and the death strip used to be. She's very intrigued by the way the city is dealing with its turbulent past, and she loves that every neighbourhood still breathes its history, and therefore feels like a village on its own. What she also loves about Berlin is how green the city still is – parks, woods, lakes, rivers and the canals take up more than 30 percent of its surface – and how open-minded the people are: in Berlin, it's all about who you are, not about how you look.

Nathalie wants to thank Dettie and Marc at Luster Publishing, whom she enjoyed working with so much. The same holds for Philipp, the photographer of this book. Also thanks to her darling Ossie-friends Swantje and Katrin, for all the info about the former GDR. She would like to apologise to her kids, Louise and Elmo, for letting her motherly duties slip a bit in sight of the deadline. And last but not least, she wants to thank the reader, for taking an interest in the wonderful city that is Berlin.

BERLIN

overview

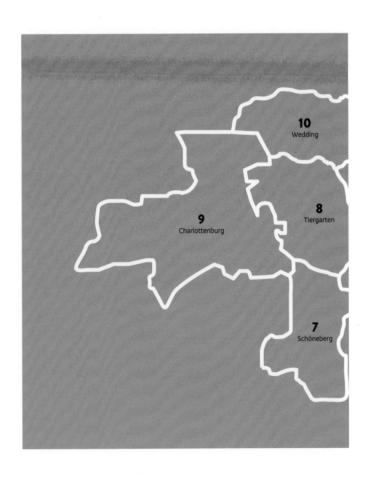

10
Wedding

8
Tiergarten

9
Charlottenburg

7
Schöneberg

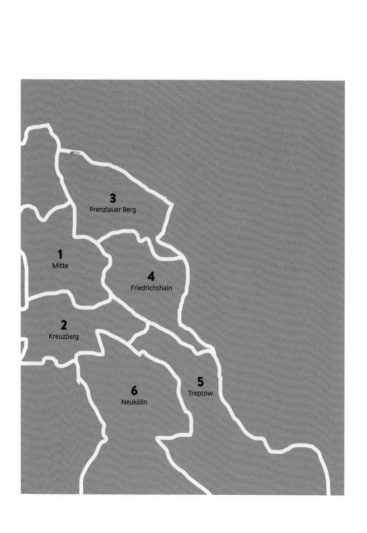

3 Prenzlauer Berg

1 Mitte

4 Friedrichshain

2 Kreuzberg

5 Treptow

6 Neukölln

Map 1

MITTE

Map 2
KREUZBERG

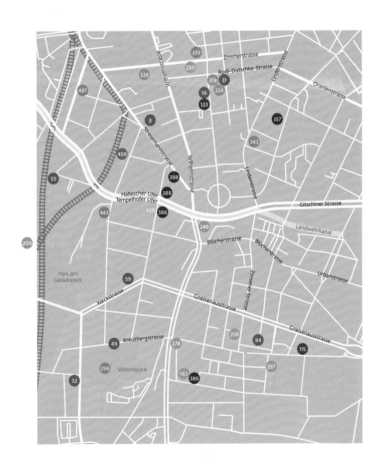

Map 3
PRENZLAUER BERG

Map 4
FRIEDRICHSHAIN

Map 5
TREPTOW

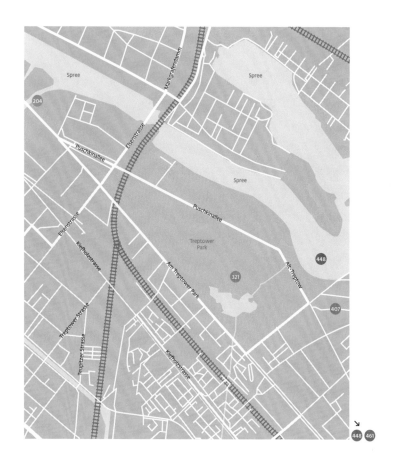

Map 6
NEUKÖLLN

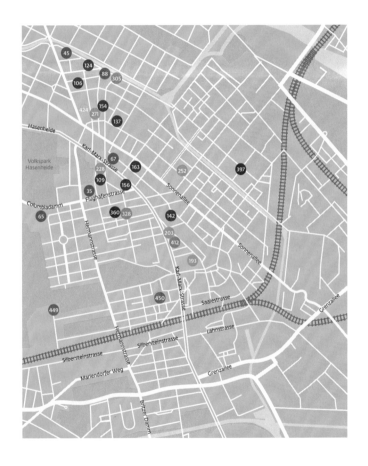

Map 7
SCHÖNEBERG

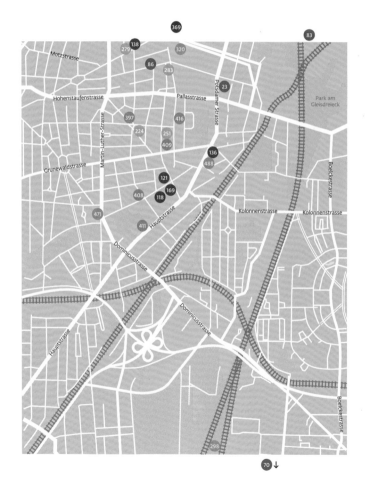

Map 8
TIERGARTEN

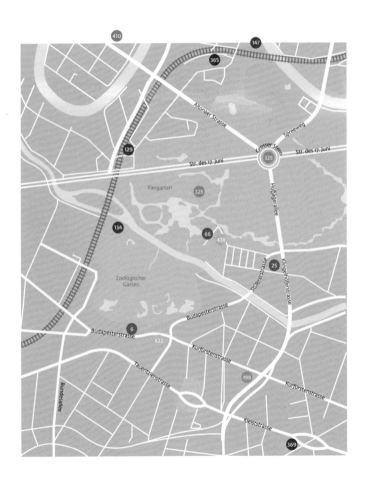

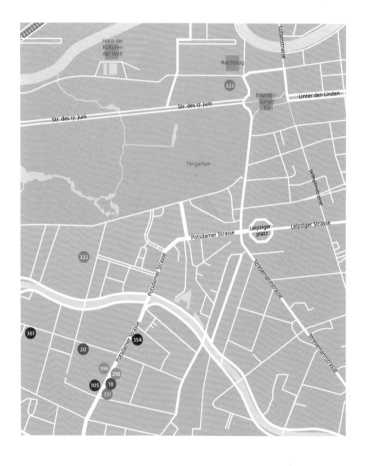

Map 9
CHARLOTTENBURG

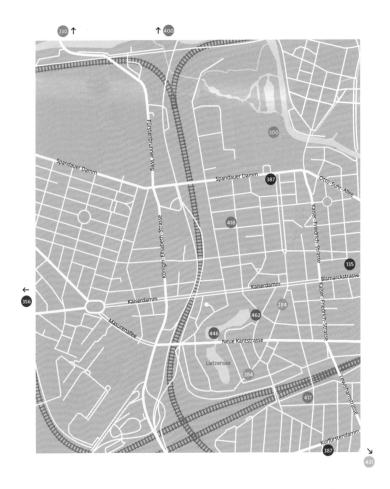

Map 10
WEDDING

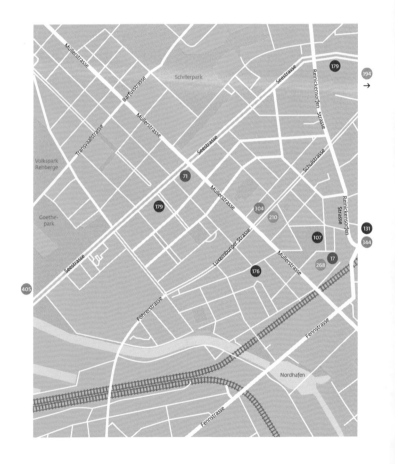

CAFÉ AM NEUEN SEE

100 PLACES
TO EAT OR BUY
GOOD FOOD

The 5 best restaurants to
EAT LIKE A BERLINER

1 **SOPHIENECK**
   Grosse Hamburger
   Strasse 37
   Mitte ①
   +49 (0)30 2834 065
   sophieneck-berlin.de

This old, cosy and often crowded establishment lies in the middle of the old Jewish neighbourhood. It offers a welcome pause after strolling around the fancy galleries in the Auguststrasse. The restaurant serves a damn good *eisbein* (pickled, usually boiled, ham) but you can also just go there for a nice beer. They host historical tours.

2 **ALTES EUROPA**
   Gipsstrasse 11
   Mitte ①
   +49 (0)30 2809 3804
   alteseuropa.com

One of the oldest bars in the neighbourhood. They also serve food and the little terrace under the tree is a very cosy place to spend a hot summer night. The menu features German food with a twist and a selection of German wines.

3 DIENER BERLIN

Grolmanstrasse 47
Charlottenburg ⑨
+49 (0)30 8815 329
diener-berlin.de

This restaurant is a real Berlin institution: it's been around for over 100 years. Expect a cosy *Kneipe*-feeling with dark walls and old pictures of local VIPs, and also some Berliner *Schnauzer* – this refers to the reputation of the Berliners of being a bit curt and brusque. They serve typical *Hausmannskost*; we recommend the *Klopse* or the eggs in mustard sauce.

4 ANABELA'S KITCHEN

Pestalozzistrasse 3
Charlottenburg ⑨
+49 (0)30 2870 1224
anabelas-kitchen.de

Here you can enjoy classic German dishes with a Portuguese twist since Anabela, the chef, was born and raised in Portugal. Her cooking is simply exquisite and the restaurant cosy and warm – think dark green colours, soft lights and handwritten recipes on the wall. Add to that the warm personality of Anabela, and you'll understand why this place is a hidden gem.

5 MAX UND MORITZ

Oranienstrasse 162
Kreuzberg ②
+49 (0)30 6951 5911
maxundmoritzberlin.de

This more than 100-years-old *Wirtshaus* (Inn) is the place to taste excellent traditional Berliner dishes like *Kutscher-gulasch* (goulash cooked with beer). Locals and tourists like the Jugendstil atmosphere. Every Sunday night, tango dancers hit the dancefloor in the wonderful ballroom in the back of the restaurant.

The 5 best
RESTAURANTS
WITH A VIEW

---

6 **NENI**

Budapester Str. 40
Tiergarten ⑧
+49 (0)30 1202 21200
neniberlin.de

Excellent Jewish food and a breathtaking view over the Zoo and over Berlin. Neni is rather difficult to find, so if you make a reservation (you should, it's popular!) ask for directions. You can have a drink first (or a coffee afterwards) in the beautiful Monkeybar on the same floor. Neni also serves a small but very affordable and delicious lunch.

9 HUGOS

7 KÄFER

Platz der Republik 1
Mitte ①
+49 (0)30 2262 990
feinkost-kaefer.de/berlin

This is the restaurant on the top floor of the Bundestag. You need to make a reservation at least 24h beforehand and don't forget to bring your passport or identity card when you go. A fantastic location and good food at a price that's not even that exaggerated.

8 SOLAR

Stresemannstr. 76
Kreuzberg ②
+49 (0)163 7652 700
solarberlin.com

A club-lounge and stylish restaurant on the 16th and 17th floor of a high building where once the cia was stationed. Chef Jon Kremin creates classic Berlin dishes but always adds a twist. The setting is wonderful, and the view is absolutely stunning.

9 HUGOS

Budapester Str. 2
Tiergarten ⑧
+49 (0)30 2602 1263
hugos-restaurant.de

This classy restaurant and wine bar offers a fantastic view over the city and a number of private dining rooms. There are three fixed menus to choose from (one of them vegetarian), and a four-course menu costs around 100 euros. Want to cook like a chef? Check out the cooking classes on their website.

10 HOTEL DE ROME

Behrenstrasse 37
Mitte ①
+49 (0)30 4606 090
roccofortehotels.com/
hotels-and-resorts/
hotel-de-rome

It doesn't get more classy and stylish than at the famous Hotel de Rome, with its amazing roof top terrace, which – few people know this – is also open to non-residents. From there you have a view on the State Opera House, St. Hedwig's Cathedral, the Berlin Cathedral and the Television Tower, just to name a few.

The 5 best
IMBISS
(fast food joints) in town

---

11 **SABZI**
   Luisenstrasse 15
   Mitte ①
   +49 (0)177 6712 732
   sabzi.de

Sabzi means 'herbs' in Persian, so it shouldn't be a surprise that this place serves lots of veggies, oriental style. The food is fresh and tasty. Actually the only thing that's typically 'fast food' here, is that you hardly have to wait for your order. No wonder that this is a popular place – meaning that it's often crowded. It's best to go either early or late. Standing room only. If you're more of a healthy breakfast person, go to CouCou in the nearby Reinhardtstrasse 37, same owners and quality.

12 **YAROK**
   Torstrasse 195
   Mitte ①
   +49 (0)30 9562 8703
   yarok-restaurant.de

This tiny Syrian restaurant serves one of the best mixed oriental plates in town. It's tasty, fresh and it's more than you can eat. The *fatush* salad is amazing. And they have a terrace on the busy and fancy street.

13 WITTY'S

Wittenbergplatz 5
Charlottenburg ⑨
+49 (0)30 6391 1666
wittys-berlin.de

Berlin has enough *Currywurst* joints to feed half the country, but Witty's stands out of that crowd. Here, they make their *Currywurst* a little different: the meat is organic and it is served with Belgian fries. The flagship store is in Charlottenburg but there are 3 different outlets, including one at BER (Berlin Brandenburg Airport).

14 IMREN GRILL

Boppstrasse 10
Kreuzberg ②
+49 (0)30 4302 7868
imren-grill.de

The döner kebab was developed in Berlin by Turkish immigrants. It's one the most popular fast foods in Berlin, and Imren is one of the best places to order one. The secret to their perfect döner? The quality of their home-baked fresh flatbread, the homemade sauces and their very special meat-marinating technique. Several branches all over Berlin.

15 W-DER IMBISS

Kastanienallee 49
Prenzlauer Berg ③
+49 (0)30 4435 2206
w-derimbiss.de

W-der Imbiss started as a healthy answer to one of the biggest burger joints in the world (look at the very recognizable upside-down M logo). This vegetarian/vegan/salmon fusion fast-food restaurant will seduce you with its healthy, super fresh and original cuisine. There's a second W in Schöneberg. You might never go M again!

5

EXQUISITE RESTAURANTS

---

16 **NOBELHART & SCHMUTZIG**

Friedrichstrasse 218
Kreuzberg ②
+49 (0)30 2594 0610
*nobelhartund
schmutzig.com*

This place and everything around is radical and young. The interior is dark but beautiful, and the food is extraordinary. The chef uses local ingredients and creates one menu for his guests, with one fixed price – there's no à la carte. His talent has already been rewarded with a Michelin star.

17 **ERNST**

Gerichtstrasse 54
Wedding ③
ernstberlin.de

This might be the city's most unorthodox restaurant: about eight seats, one menu, one Michelin star, one Canadian culinary prodigy, zero compromises. Little brother JULIUS across the street is a nice (and cheaper) alternative if you don't want to reserve months in advance.

18 **PANAMA**

Potsdamer Strasse 91
Tiergarten ⑧
+49 (0)30 9832 08435
oh-panama.com

You will immediately feel at home in this stylish restaurant, which is tucked away in a hidden courtyard on the upcoming Potsdamer Strasse. Chef Sophia Rudolph has put together a short but quite interesting menu with an exotic twist that also includes raw dishes for example. Don't forget to order a cocktail at the bar on the ground floor!

19 LE PETIT ROYAL

Grolmanstrasse 59
Charlottenburg ⑨
+49 (0)30 3300 60750
lepetitroyal.de

The restaurant stands for classical French cuisine with an emphasis on steaks and fish. Also the wine menu, featuring mostly French wines, is very good. The interior is classy, with lots of contemporary art. And there's a lovely summer terrace.

20 KIN DEE

Lützowstrasse 81
Tiergarten ⑧
+49 (0)30 2155 294
kindeeberlin.com

Chef Dalad Kambhu and her crew aim to serve traditional Thai food with a local twist. To achieve their goal, they mix classical ingredients with regionally sourced products – for example, they'll use koolrabi instead of papaya. The result is truly delicious. In 2021 Kin Dee received a Michelin star for the third consecutive year.

16 NOBELHART & SCHMUTZIG

5 places to enjoy a
PERFECT LUNCH

---

21 MONSIEUR VUONG
**Alte Schönhauser
Strasse 46**
Mitte ①
+49 (0)30 9929 6924
monsieurvuong.de

In need of a break after a shopping spree in the fancy Alte Schönhauser Strasse? How about a Vietnamese lunch? Monsieur Vuong is a safe bet: always hip, always authentic and yes, also always crowded. Bright colours and friendly service have been its trademark since 1999.

22 CAFÉ-RESTAURANT WINTERGARTEN IM LITERATURHAUS
Fasanenstrasse 23
Charlottenburg ⑨
+49 (0)30 8825 414
literaturhaus-berlin.de

This legendary institution also houses the exquisite bookstore Kohlhaas & Company. It's a fantastic place to go to after a day of shopping or to have afternoon tea – when the weather is nice, you can enjoy your tea in the spacious garden. They also organise walking tours.

23 MALAKEH
Potsdamer Str. 153
Schöneberg ⑦
+49 (0)176 2216 0998
malakeh-restaurant.de

Malakeh Jazmati, born in Damascus, came to Berlin in 2015 after living in exile in Jordan, where she had her own cooking show on TV. She started a catering business in Berlin that was so good that she was soon asked by none other than Angela Merkel to serve Syrian food at a reception. Not much later, she opened Malakeh – a real gem of a Syrian restaurant.

24 MARIA BONITA

Danziger Strasse 33
Prenzlauer Berg ③
+49 (0)176 3652 6955
mariabonita.de

If you're craving hearty Mexican food in Berlin, look no further. Maria Bonita is a small cantina that serves tasty Frozen Mezcal Margaritas and excellent homemade *chilaquiles*. It's not exactly light fare, but it will get you going. Explore the neighbourhood (with the famous Kulturbrauerei around the corner) until it's time for dinner.

25 NORDISCHE BOTSCHAFTEN

Rauchstrasse 1
Tiergarten ⑧
+49 (0)30 50500
nordische botschaften.org

It is a little-known Berlin fact that many local organisations have canteens that are open to the public. Often they serve decent food at a decent price. Universal's cantina in Friedrichshain is a good example. Fans of Nordic architecture can try the canteen of the Felleshus – a cultural space run by five Nordic institutions.

25 NORDISCHE BOTSCHAFTEN

5 excellent
MEAT RESTAURANTS

---

26 **LUTTER & WEGNER**
   Charlottenstrasse 56
   Mitte ①
   +49 (0)30 2029 5415
   l-w-berlin.de

It feels like this restaurant has been around forever. It is situated on the fantastic Gendarmenmarkt where tourists and local businessmen meet. Their *Wiener Schnitzel* is legendary and comes in two sizes. It's served with the typical lukewarm potato-cucumber salad or with crispy *Bratkartoffeln*.

27 **GRILL ROYAL**
   Friedrichstrasse 105-B
   Mitte ①
   +49 (0)3 0288 79288
   grillroyal.com

Grill Royal not only serves excellent meat dishes like Entrecote Pomerinia or T-bone steak but also lobster, oysters and other seafood. The place is known as the restaurant of the stars, so you might be lucky and have dinner with George Clooney.

28 USHIDO

Lychener Strasse 18
Prenzlauer Berg ③
+49 (0)30 5524 2448
ushido-bbq.com

The team behind this restaurant has an interesting goal: to help people eat healthy by introducing them to the Japanese cuisine. Their lunch (in bento boxes i.e.) is extremely balanced and the meat that features on the dinner menu is of excellent quality. First yakiniku restaurant in Berlin.

29 FLEISCHEREI

Schönhauser Allee 8
Prenzlauer Berg ③
+49 (0)30 5018 2117
fleischerei-berlin.com

A beautiful old butcher shop transformed into an even more beautiful restaurant situated on the hip Schönhauser Allee. They serve high-quality German meat classics and excellent, mostly Austrian wines. The special lunch menu is cheap and changes almost daily.

30 FLEISCHEREI DOMKE

Warschauer Str. 64
Friedrichshain ④
+49 (0)30 2917 635
fleischereidomke.de

If you're looking for an unpretentious snack that will not let you down, you've found it. This butcher is a real Berlin institution. Don't expect light dishes, subtle flavours, a fancy interior or vegan desserts, because this is old-school German food, *Sauerkraut* included. Prices start at 1 euro for a sandwich with *Wurst*.

The 5 best
ITALIAN
restaurants

---

31 SALE E TABACCHI
Rudi-Dutschke-Str. 25
Kreuzberg ②
+49 (0)30 2521 155
sale-e-tabacchi.de

This restaurant just around the corner of Checkpoint Charlie is much loved by the arty crowd and journalists who work in the neighbourhood. It serves mainly traditional Italian dishes and they do have a daily changing menu. The scenery is great: the 6-metre-high, mostly blue coloured walls were designed by Swiss architect Max Dudler.

32 RIPIENO
Monumentenstr. 21
Kreuzberg ②
+49 (0)157 8133 2108

Damn good coffee and cake in this tiny establishment across from the beautiful Viktoriapark. They also serve homemade pasta and the owners are incredibly sweet. If you can't find what you're looking for here, try In Cibus across the street or have a cocktail at Pavlov's Bar down the road.

33 CAPVIN

Weinbergsweg 24
Mitte ①
+49 (0)30 4404 7080
capvin.de/berlin

It is possible to open a crazy successful restaurant in the midst of a pandemic, and Capvin is here to prove it. Neapolitan pizza master and wonderboy Vincenzo Capuano added some really unique pizzas to his menu. Try for example *Patata di Viola* that comes with *Fior di Latte*, purple potato crisps, rosemary, parmesan cream and basil. *Buon appetito!*

34 AL CONTADINO SOTTO LE STELLE

Auguststrasse 36
Mitte ①
+49 (0)30 2819 023
alcontadino.eu/restaurant

The delicious dishes you can try at this cosy traditional Italian restaurant are mostly inspired by the Basilicata region. The menu changes every month and features, among other things, home made pasta and excellent focaccia. If you like high quality and fresh buffalo mozzarella, then visit the Mozzarella Bar and Botega of the same owners in the same street.

35 LAVANDERIA VECCHIA

Flughafenstrasse 46
Neukölln ⑥
+49 (0)30 6272 2152
lavanderiavecchia.de

This isn't the most beautiful street in the world, but you'll forget all about it once you see the backyard: you will feel as if you were in a southern Italian city. Special diets must be communicated beforehand and you can't make reservations. The owners opened a second restaurant, Lava, where the prices are lower.

5 must-visit restaurants for
VEGETARIANS

---

36 **COOKIES CREAM**

Behrenstrasse 55
Mitte ①
+49 (0)30 2749 2940
cookiescream.com

This posh place has something secret about it: guests aren't allowed to take photos inside, and it's a bit hard to find – you have to take a look on their website for hints about the location. Maybe that's part of the reason why it attracts a fashion crowd. Also, the food is extremely good (and doesn't come cheap). There's always one vegan option. The owners also have the equally excellent restaurant Crackers. One Michelin Star.

37 **BISTRO BARDOT**

Boxhagenerstr. 83
Friedrichshain ④
+49 (0)30 6920 97082
bistrobardot.de

The bistro of the (bio)hotel Almodovar in trendy Friedrichshain is light and friendly. The limited but creative menu features mostly Mediterranean dishes, made with organic and fresh ingredients. They offer a very good Sunday brunch at a reasonable price. Check out the nice backyard.

38 MOMOS

Chausseestrasse 2
Mitte ①
+49 (0)160 2688 177
momos-berlin.de

Momos are typical Himalayan dumplings, and this restaurant takes them to a next level: all the ingredients are strictly organic and everything is home made. Try the 'Momo experience' to taste all eight *momos* and their dips. Order at the bar (like in many other Berlin's establishments). Open daily. Also take-away.

39 ATAYA CAFFE

Zelterstrasse 6
Prenzlauer Berg ③
atayavegan.com

Elisabette (a chef born in Sardinia) and Bachir (a musician born in Senegal) are the owners of this lovely living-room-style cafe in fancy Prenzlauer Berg. A unique place where Italy meets Africa and where the plates are as colourful as that mix sounds. Their Sunday brunch is to die for, but make sure to make a reservation a few days ahead to be sure of a spot.

40 RESTAURANT 1990

Krossener Str. 19
Friedrichshain ④
+49 (0)30 8561 4761
restaurant1990.de

Berlin's culinary scene represents a sheer number of cultures and this number is still increasing. Restaurant 1990 is one of the newcomers. It serves one of the best vegan Vietnamese tapas in town in a great ambience. Tip: order a myriad of their adorable little bowls. Every single one not only looks fabulous, but even tastes better.

5 places that
MAKE YOU GO VEGAN
in a second

---

41 VAUST BRAUGASTSTATTE

Pestalozzistrasse 8
Charlottenburg ⑨
+49 (0)30 5459 9160
vaust.berlin

Vaust is one of the few fancy 100 percent vegan restaurants in Berlin. The service is friendly and the cuisine could be classified as 'vegan German fine dining'. Portions are rather small so you still have some room for the very tasty chocolate cake. Another plus: they have self-brewed beer.

42 KOPPS

Linienstrasse 94
Mitte ①
+49 (0)30 4320 9775
kopps-berlin.de

Kopps has been around since 2011 and CNN voted it one of the best vegan restaurants in the world. The restaurant emphasises quality, regional produce sourced from small farmers in Brandenburg. They also serve an excellent brunch in the weekends. Lots of good coffee bars and ice-cream parlours in the neighbourhood.

43 SOY

Rosa-Luxemburg-
Strasse 30
Mitte ①
+49 (0)30 2340 5890
soy-berlin.com

Very tasty glutamate-free dishes at very reasonable prices: that's what you can expect at this beautiful restaurant near the Babylon cinema. The restaurant was designed with the help of a feng-shui master and has a nice view on the Volksbühne and an outside terrace.

44 LUCKY LEEK

Kollwitzstrasse 54
Prenzlauer Berg ③
+49 (0)30 6640 8710
lucky-leek.com

Here's one of the first vegan restaurants that took vegan food to another level. It's located right between the Kollwitzplatz and the famous Water Tower and offers a superb dining experience. It's a little on the expensive side for Berlin but Josita Hartanto's vegan dishes are worth it – think pear and chilli risotto with *tandoori* cabbage and *nori tempeh* rolls. Nice outside terrace.

45 BRAMMIBAL'S DONUTS

Maybachufer 8
Neukölln ⑥
+49 (0)30 2394 8455
brammibalsdonuts.com

Situated opposite the canal in trendy Kreuzkölln, this is donut heaven for those with a sweet tooth! Available in wildly creative flavours, these veganised donuts are a gift to Berlin and to humanity. The maple smoked coconut one is our favourite. Order it with one of their speciality coffees and enjoy.

45 BRAMMIBAL'S DONUTS

The 5 places where you should try
A TYPICAL
BERLINER BRUNCH

---

46 **CAFÉ MORGENROT**
Kastanienallee 85
Prenzlauer Berg ③
+49 (0)30 4431 7844
morgenrot.blogsport.eu

One of the last authentic spots on the heavily gentrified Kastanienallee. There used to be a lot of open venues called *Kollektiv* in Berlin but unfortunately, they are quickly disappearing. Café Morgenrot still (but barely!) survives. They serve a very good and cheap brunch at the weekend. Bring your punk attitude!

48 SILO COFFEE

47 CAFÉ MUGRABI

Görlitzer Strasse 58
Kreuzberg ②
+49 (0)30 2658 5400
cafemugrabi.com

In summer, the entire area around Görlitzer Park feels like one big party zone. One of the nicest places for a post-clubbing breakfast or a Sunday brunch is Café Mugrabi. The food is inspired by the Israeli and North-African cuisine. Try the *shakshuka* (a special tomato dish with poached eggs) and the hummus, they are delicious.

48 SILO COFFEE

Gabriel-Max-Strasse 4
Friedrichshain ④
silo-coffee.com

Silo produces speciality coffee and is an ideal place to go before or after strolling around the flea market on the Boxhagener Platz. It's one of the few really good breakfast places in Friedrichshain.

49 TOMASA VILLA KREUZBERG

Kreuzbergstrasse 62
Kreuzberg ②
+49 (0)30 8100 9885
tomasa.de/tomasa-restaurant/tomasa-villa-kreuzberg-berlin

Tomasa has been elected as one of the best breakfast restaurants in Berlin by Prinz magazine. The nineteenth-century red brick fairytale villa is located near the fantastic Victoriapark and it also has a beautiful courtyard and view on a little zoo. It's also extremely child friendly.

50 BENEDICT

Uhlandstrasse 49
Charlottenburg ⑨
+49 (0)30 9940 40997
benedict-breakfast.de

Benedict was already an über-cool breakfast-only place in Tel-Aviv when the owners decided to open a branch in Berlin. It's located on the ground floor of the hip Max Brown hotel. Their eggs Benedict are - unsurprisingly - legendary. The place is insanely popular and they don't take reservations but you can order picnic boxes. Open 8:30 till 15:30, Friday to Sunday 8:00 till 15:00.

5 restaurants
HIPSTERS *will love*

---

51 TULUS LOTREK

Fichtestrasse 24
Kreuzberg ②
+49 (0)30 4195 6687
tuluslotrek.de

Good ol' Toulouse-Lautrec would turn in his grave when he saw how his name was corrupted but chances are he would appreciate the food and the surroundings. Epicurean Belle Époque meets modern cuisine in this contemporary restaurant, where recognizable ingredients are the key. One Michelin Star.

52 893 RYŌTEI

Kantstrasse 135
Charlottenburg ⑨
+49 (0)30 9170 3121
893ryotei.de

Once you find the entrance of this restaurant in West-Berlin – it's hidden, which is very East-Berlin-like – you'll step into the science fiction world of the legendary Berliner restaurateur The Duc Ngo. Here you'll find Asian fusion cooking at its best, tattooed staff, superb decoration.

53 ZOLA

Paul-Lincke-Ufer 39-40
Kreuzberg ②
+49 (0)151 4359 6561

Zola opened in December 2015 and its Neapolitan-style pizza was an instant hit. With its massive, wood-fired oven, Zola dishes out some of the tastiest pizza Berlin has ever seen. Order at the bar. After your pizza frenzy, try next door's coffee bar called 'Concierge' for a double shot espresso.

54 LODE & STIJN

Lausitzerstrasse 25
Kreuzberg ②
+49 (0)30 6521 4507
lode-stijn.de

You thought Dutchies couldn't cook? Think again and try out the food at this Dutch restaurant! They stand for seasonal cooking, a few Dutch classics like *bitterballen* (meatballs), and a very good value four-or six-course menu.

55 BRLO BRWHOUSE

Schöneberger Str. 16
Kreuzberg ②
+49 (0)30 5557 7606
brlo-brwhouse.de

Take 38 upcycled shipping containers, a brewery, a unique location in the Gleisdreieck park, add some passionate people to that mix *et voilà*: a hotspot for foodies and contemporary craft beer geeks is born. Vegetables – fermented, smoked, dehydrated, smoked or fried – have the starring role in chef Ben Pommer's dishes. Superb beer garden.

54 LODE & STIJN

5 nice places for
CAKE LOVERS

---

56 PASTEL

Wrangelstrasse 44
Kreuzberg ②
+49 (0)30 5497 8129
bekarei.de

This super tiny Portuguese bakery is the little sister of the big Bekarei in Prenzlauer Berg. Georgios and Paula only serve baked goods from Greece and of course Portugal, so this is the place to try a *pastel de nata*. If you can't decide what pastel to take, you can try them all, because they're available in mini-sizes.

57 AUNT BENNY

Oderstrasse 7
(Enter: Jessnerstr.)
Friedrichshain ④
+49 (0)30 6640 5300
auntbenny.com

Aunt Benny is basically a cafe run by two Canadian siblings and located opposite a park with a playground. It's an ideal place to sip (very good) coffee, have a home-baked cake and watch the children play. All baked goods can be ordered and brunch is served on Sunday. Very good gluten-free and vegan options as well.

58 BLACK APRON

Invalidenstrasse 1
Mitte ①
+49 (0)30 9146 9449
blackapron-bakery.com

In the midst of hipster Berlin, on the corner of Invalidenstrasse and Brunnenstrasse, you will find this big, beautiful, and always crowded bakery. They have their own coffee brand CODOS, which is sourced and roasted by them too. Our favourite cake is called 'Death by Chocolate'. Bam!

59 MR. MINSCH

Yorckstrasse 15
Kreuzberg ②
+49 (0)30 5266 4903
mr-minsch-torten.de

Mr. Minsch offers a daily selection of up to twenty classical tortes, cakes and fancy cakes. Some of those are very special, very Berlin-like creations – this means they're a bit kinky and weird. You can buy a cake to take home or enjoy a piece with a coffee. Trust us, you won't be able to resist all these absolutely fabulous-looking treats.

60 JUBEL

Hufelandstrasse 10
Prenzlauer Berg ③
+49 (0)30 5521 6150
jubel-berlin.de

Situated in the cosy Hufelandstrasse in leafy Prenzlauer Berg, this place is a real heaven if you have a sweet tooth. Kai Michels and Lucie Babinska are passionate about their work and their delicate and delicious creations are absolutely worth a visit. Whether you want a whole cake for a birthday, a huge wedding *Torte*, or just some small cupcakes, this is the place to go.

The 5 best
KOREAN
restaurants

---

61 **KOREAN FOOD STORIES**
Prenzlauer Allee 217
Prenzlauer Berg ③
+49 (0)157 3637 5002
koreanfoodstories.com

Korean food has been extremely popular in Berlin for a while and now it's slowly but surely conquering the rest of the world. We understand why: the tastes are bold and pure and most of the food is extremely healthy because a lot of the ingredients are fermented. If you want to dive into the world of the different *kimchi* flavours, Korean Food Stories is the perfect place to start.

62 **KIMCHI PRINCESS**
Skalitzer Strasse 36
Kreuzberg ②
+49 (0)163 4580 203
kimchiprincess.com

Sizzling grills, young and beautiful people, loud music, a pretty good bibimbap and a massive choice of *kimchi*… This Korean restaurant is buzzy and exciting, and the ideal starting point for a night out with friends. Same owners as Angry Chicken in Kreuzberg and Mani Mono in Adlersdorf.

63 DAE MON

Monbijouplatz 11
Mitte ①
+49 (0)30 2630 4811
dae-mon.com

It doesn't get any fancier than this –
or more stylish, or darker. Design chairs,
light installations, big photos on dark
walls... This contemporary Korean
restaurant is all about style, all the way,
thanks to Felix Pahnke, who redesigned
the interior in 2016. And best of all:
the look matches the quality of the food –
it's exquisite. Not the cheapest place to
go for dinner, but if you want to impress
your date, Dae Mon is a must!

64 YAM YAM

Alte Schönhauserstr. 6
Mitte ①
+49 (0)30 2463 2485
yamyam-berlin.de

Here you can enjoy an excellent kimchi
soup at a fair price. During lunch Yam
Yam is often crowded so try to go after
2 pm. The restaurant is super cosy and
small, and it's close to the fantastic
Rosa-Luxemburg-Platz with its cool shops
and galleries.

65 MMAAH

Columbiadamm 160
Neukölln ⑥
+49 (0)176 9309 0623
mmaah.de

Once a shabby shack on the corner of the
Tempelhofer Feld, now a hip and yummy
take-away restaurant in Tempelhof Park,
serving Korean street food prepared
with mostly local vegetables and meat.
The location is unique, seeing that this
is the site of the Berlin Airlift: during the
Cold War, western countries flew in food
and supplies by plane, because all other
routes to Berlin were blocked by the
Soviet Union. Two other restaurants:
one in Neukölln and one in Schöneberg.

5 restaurants with a
LOVELY GARDEN TERRACE

---

66 **CAFÉ AM NEUEN SEE**
Lichtensteinallee 2
Tiergarten ⑧
+49 (0)30 2544 930
cafeamneuensee.de

After visiting the Reichstag and the Brandenburg Gate, go for a stroll in the Tiergarten and enjoy a bite or a beer at Café am Neuen See. Hidden secret: walk to the Tiergarten S-Bahn station and have a look at the 90 beautiful historic gas lanterns (from Berlin and other cities) that are on display outdoors for everyone to enjoy. They are illuminated at dusk.

67 **NOLA'S AM WEINBERG**
Veteranenstrasse 9
Mitte ①
+49 (0)30 4404 0766
nolas.de

This pavilion from the fifties has a fantastic terrace overlooking the Weinberg Park near the fancy Rosenthalerplatz. It's open all day, serving Swiss dishes – including different fondues – and brunch on Sunday. There are some good vegan and gluten-free options.

68 WIRTSHAUS ZUR PFAUENINSEL

Pfaueninsel-
chaussee 100
Wannsee
+49 (0)30 8052 225
pfaueninsel.de

This beer garden may be a little further away from the city centre but it's easy to get to by S-Bahn and bus. Your trip will be worth it, not because of the food per se – it's good but not too refined – but because of the fantastic location with a view over the Pfaueninsel (peacock island). After your meal, you can take the ferry and visit the 70-hectares-big island to say hi to the peacocks.

69 SCHOENBRUNN

Volkspark
Friedrichshain
Friedrichshain ④
+49 (0)30 4530 56525
schoenbrunn.net

Another restaurant and beer garden in a big and beautiful park. It's a huge place, so not really hidden, but because it's in the middle of the park, you can easily miss it if you don't know it's there. On the menu you'll find pizzas and the omnipresent *Currywurst*.

70 BERGTERRASSE MARIENHÖHE

Marienhöher Weg 30
Tempelhof
+49 (0)30 7532 839
*bergterrasse-
marienhoehe.de*

This wonderful garden is the place to go if you want to enjoy classic German dishes without hipsters around. This restaurant attracts locals who come here for a nice beer or a *Kaffee mit Kuchen*. Sometimes that's all you need on a beautiful hot summer day.

The 5 best
A S I A N
restaurants

---

71 ASIA DELI
Seestrasse 41
Wedding ③
+49 (0)30 9144 1925
asia-deli.eatbu.com

Definitely not a restaurant for a first date, but worth a visit if you're into authentic Chinese food. If you look European you will get the standard, blander menu, so be sure to ask for the Chinese version if you can take the heat. Authentic Hunan dishes, hot and spicy – just the way we like them.

72 RYONG
Torstrasse 59
Mitte ①
+49 (0)30 30 30 70 47
ryong.de

Ryong stands for sophisticated street food. This Vietnamese-Japanese restaurant serves homemade noodles and excellent bao burgers, all vegetarian or vegan. The menu is concise and the trendy, design atmosphere is stunning. There is a second location in Prenzlauer Berg.

73 LONG MARCH CANTEEN
Wrangelstrasse 20
Kreuzberg ②
+49 (0)178 8849 599
longmarchcanteen.com

A splendid and modern looking Chinese restaurant with an open kitchen. The menu features sophisticated dumplings and more. For dessert, try the caramelised hot bananas that come with a bowl of ice water. You should dunk the banana in for a few seconds so that the outside turns crispy while the inside stays soft: it's so delicious.

74 LON-MEN'S NOODLE HOUSE

Kantstrasse 33
Charlottenburg ⑨
+49 (0)30 3151 9678

The Kantstrasse is becoming more and more popular as an alternative to the Kurfürstendamm just around the corner. If you want to try Taiwanese food you came to the right spot: Lon-Men's Noodle House is probably the only Taiwanese restaurant in the city. The food is authentic, fast and a healthy alternative for the good ol' *Currywurst*.

75 FEEL SEOUL GOOD

Husemannstrasse 2
Prenzlauer Berg ③
+49 (0)30 4749 6766

Korean vegan soul food on the corner of trendy Kollwitzplatz and Husemann-strasse with a lovely sunny terrace. Unlike many other Asian restaurants, they have a rather short menu, which is always a good sign. Prices are average considering it's Prenzlauer Berg and the portions are more than generous. Excellent ramyun soups and great *bibimbap*!

73 LONG MARCH CANTEEN

5

STUNNING
RESTAURANTS

---

76 **CRACKERS**
Friedrichstrasse 158
Mitte ①
+49 (0)30 6807 30488
crackersberlin.com

The once famous Cookies Club in Mitte has been transformed into a super cool restaurant with high-quality Charolais beef dishes on the menu. Crackers is the latest venture of Heinz Gindullis, the food entrepreneur who has given the Berliners yummy vegetarian options like Chipps and Cookies Cream. There are DJ dinner sets on Fridays and Saturdays.

77 **CUMBERLAND RESTAURANT**
Kurfürstendamm 194
Charlottenburg ⑨
+49 (0)30 2769 6308
cumberland-restaurant.de

The Cumberland building has a long history that not every Berliner is aware of. Entering the Cumberland Restaurant or their wine bar is like stepping into another era. We especially love to sit on the terrace in summer. Expect classic French Cuisine with a modern twist. Open Tuesday till Saturday from 12:00 till 15:00 and from 18:30. Wine bar 15:00 - 22:00.

78 THE GRAND

Hirtenstrasse 4
Mitte ①
+49 (0)30 2789 09 9555
the-grand-berlin.com

A restaurant, bar and club in one. The restaurant is specialised in beef dishes and offers a lunch *menu du jour* and a vegetarian dish or grill of the week. The old-school swing bar serves excellent drinks and a nice selection of cigars. And if you feel the need to go clubbing, just go upstairs to their equally stylish club and party on.

79 ORA

Oranienplatz 14
Kreuzberg ②
ora-berlin.de

A former pharmacy built in 1860, turned into a modern bar and restaurant. A bit on the expensive side, but lunch and dinner are absolutely worth it. Excellent wine list too, which is rare in Berlin. The Ora experience is pretty complete: an abundance of pharmacy memorabilia, cosy leather couches, fresh, mostly organic and vibrant food, superb pastry and excellent signature cocktails. What's not to like?

80 PAULY SAAL

Auguststrasse 11-13
Mitte ①
+49 (0)30 3300 6070
paulysaal.com

Everything about this restaurant is classy: the building, the chairs, the chandelier, the drinks, the clients, and the inner courtyard. Housed in a former Jewish girls' school in the heart of Mitte, this is a fantastic place to dine or just to sip a cocktail at the bar. Be sure to visit the Eigen Art Gallery on the third floor of the same building.

5 irresistible
INDOOR STREET FOOD
MARKETS *and* TRUCKS

---

81 **MARKTHALLE 9**
Eisenbahnstr. 42-43
Kreuzberg ②
+49 (0)30 6107 3473
markthalleneun.de

This is a usual suspect for the Berlin foodies, with a cantina and bar that are open from Monday to Saturday. Thursday is Street Food Day and there are big markets on Fridays and Saturdays. The products sold here are mostly locally sourced from small-scale producers. Some really good bakeries are represented here too: Sironi, to name just one!

82 **STREET FOOD AUF ACHSE**
Kulturbrauerei
Sredzkistrasse 1
Prenzlauer Berg ③
+49 (0)30 4431 0737
streetfoodaufachse.de

A classic street food market in the courtyards of the old and beautiful brewery called Kulturbrauerei. Entrance is free and nothing should cost more than 5 euros. Come with an empty stomach, the food is delicious! Open every Sunday from 12 pm on, winter and summer.

83 **BITE CLUB**
AT: JULES B-PART
AM GLEISDREIECK PARK
Luckenwalder Str. 6-B
Schöneberg ⑦
biteclub.de

At the Bite Club street food party you can enjoy excellent local food and ditto drinks in a club-like atmosphere. It is located in front of the Café Jules in the Gleisdreieckpark and if you arrive before 7 pm entrance is free.

84 **MARHEINEKE MARKTHALLE**
Marheinekeplatz /
Bergmannstrasse
Kreuzberg ②
+49 (0)30 5056 6536
meine-markthalle.de

This market is less of a hipster hangout than the first two. It's open every day of the week except on Sunday. Most of the food you'll find here is organic and local. And if you prefer to sit in the sun and enjoy your food at a proper table: restaurant Matzbach has a big terrace.

85 **SHAWARMA MAMA**
Different food
markets in Berlin

Chef Arie Oshri is the king of Tel Aviv street food by day and a renowned drag queen by night in Berlin's (in)famous clubs. He is assisted by Kanaan's chef Gheiath Khowais, a Syrian refugee. This is *shawarma* (= döner) on a whole new level!

81 MARKTHALLE 9

5 *beautiful*
OUTDOOR OLD-SCHOOL FOOD MARKETS

---

86 **WINTERFELDTMARKT**
Winterfeldtstrasse
Schöneberg ⑦
+49 (0)175 4374 303

This beautiful farmers' market takes place on Saturday. Take the opportunity to stroll around the nice surroundings when you're there: maybe you can take a look at the Hochbunker in the Pallaststrasse, built by prisoners of the Nazis. Or you can stroll through the hip and less hip picturesque streets of Schöneberg.

87 **KOLLWITZMARKT**
Kollwitzplatz
Prenzlauer Berg ③
+49 (0)172 3278 238

This organic farmers' market is yummie and yuppie; this is Prenzlauer Berg after all. Despite the 'Prenzl' Berg-haters' it is still a pleasure to stroll around this gentrified area with its beautiful streets – with equally beautiful houses and lots of trees, cool terraces and nice bars, middle class people, and lots of kids. The market takes place every Thursday.

88 TURKISH MARKET

Maybachufer
Neukölln ⑥
tuerkenmarkt.de

You can buy cheap vegetables, fruits and fabrics here every Tuesday and Friday from 11 am tot 6.30 pm. In summertime, take the U-bahn to Schönleinstrasse and stroll along the canals while listening to some pretty good buskers. Oh, and don't forget to buy falafels on the market, they are superb.

89 BOXHAGENER PLATZ FARMERS MARKET

Friedrichshain ④
+49 (0)178 4762 242
boxhagenerplatz.org

This wonderful market in the former East Berlin has some great stalls – try TofuTussis' handmade tofu for example. Open every Thursday but closed on public holidays. Same Platz, different markets on Saturday (mainly food but some nice artisan stalls as well) and Sunday (flea market).

90 KARL-AUGUSTPLATZ

Charlottenburg ⑨
+49 (0)30 9029 29072

This market in posh Charlottenburg might be less hip than the ones above, but it's more authentic. It takes place on Wednesday and on Saturday mornings. The stalls around the Trinitatis church sell lots of fruit and veggies (mostly organic), Neuland meat and a pretty large variety of flowers.

The 5 best places for
HUMMUS *and/or*
FALAFEL

---

91 **DADA FALAFEL**
   Linienstrasse 132
   Mitte ①
   +49 (0)30 2759 6927
   dadafalafel.de

Dada Falafel is still one of the best falafel places in town. Enjoy your chickpeas with a mixed orange-and-carrot juice (ask for it, it's not on the menu) and voilà, there you have a healthy, cheap and super tasty meal. Also, there's a big and sunny terrace.

92 **HUMMUS AND FRIENDS**
   Oranienburger Str. 27
   Mitte ①
   +49 (0)30 5547 1454
   hummus-and-friends.com

"Make hummus not walls": that's what's written on one of the walls of this kosher and almost vegan restaurant, with its olivewood interior and a huge terrace in the backyard. It's not the cheapest place in this list and they specialise in hummus, so there is no falafel. Try their menu with three different kinds of hummus; you won't regret it.

93 **MO'S KLEINER IMBISS**
AKA THE KING OF FALAFEL
Urbanstrasse 68
Kreuzberg ②

In an uneventful part of the mostly sizzling Kreuzberg, you'll find the King of Falafel. He didn't get this nickname without reason, so be prepared to queue. Seating is limited, so most people simply enjoy their delicious *Falafel im Brot* (vegan or with cheese), outside.

94 **KANAAN**
Schliemannstrasse 15
Prenzlauer Berg ③
+49 (0)30 5771 41599
kanaan-berlin.de

The Israeli-Palestinian food here is amazing, and the hummus is one of the best in town. The place is popular with Instagrammers and the owner himself is enthusiastic about the food he serves, which adds to the charm. Also take-away.

95 **ZULA**
Husemannstrasse 10
Prenzlauer Berg ③
+49 (0)30 4171 5100
zulaberlin.com

Establishments in the Husemannstrasse are always a little fancy and posh and Zula is no exception. The focus lies on the hummus but they serve it with beans, with tomatoes, with goulash, chicken or with vegetables. They also serve an excellent *sabich* (fresh pita bread filled with hummus and eggplant), and there's a very nice terrace on the quiet leafy street.

The 5 best

TURKISH

restaurants

---

96 **OSMANS TÖCHTER**
Pappelallee 15
Prenzlauer Berg ①
+49 (0)30 3266 3388
osmanstoechter.de

Most Turkish restaurants in Berlin stand for döner kebab – which was invented in Berlin – and maybe some Turkish pizza. It's pretty rare to find a beautiful, trendy and modern Turkish restaurant in the city, but here is one. They recently opened a second restaurant with the same name in Charlottenburg.

97 **DEFNE**
Planufer 92-C
Kreuzberg ②
+49 (0)30 8179 7111
defne-restaurant.de

This small but wonderful restaurant lies on the lovely Planufer near the Landwehrkanal. They serve classic Anatolian dishes using authentic ingredients from the local Turkish market on the other *Ufer* (shore) of the canal. Only open for dinner.

98 **HONÇA**
Ludwichkirchplatz 12
Charlottenburg ⑨
+49 (0)30 2393 9114
honca.de

A Turkish haven in a neighbourhood that doesn't have that many Turkish restaurants or inhabitants. Here you can taste traditional Anatolian dishes without much ado – also in the nice-looking interior of the restaurant, there's no room for kitsch. Service is friendly.

99 HASIR

(6 locations)
+49 (0)30 6150 7080
hasir.de

When the Turkish immigrants came to Berlin in the eighties, they brought their food culture with them. Their use of vegetables and olive oil was totally new for the Germans, but it really influenced and enriched the heavy German cuisine. Hasir is an exemplary restaurant when it comes to Turkish food. It started very small, but now there are six Hasir restaurants in Berlin.

100 GÖZLEME

Karl-Marx-Strasse 35
Neukölln ⑥
+49 (0)30 6134 134

The Karl Marx Strasse is a very busy street in the popular Neukölln area where there is no shortage of Turkish restaurants. Don't be fooled by the cheap-looking exterior of Gözleme: this food is the real thing! Everything, including the *manti* (Turkish dumplings) is freshly prepared. An ideal place to go before heading to a party at the Klunkerkranich rooftop bar in the same street.

KREUZBERG

80 PLACES TO GO FOR A DRINK

———

5 amazing
COCKTAIL BARS
with a zest of Berlin

---

101 BUCK AND BRECK

Brunnenstrasse 177
Mitte ①
+49 (0)176 3231 5507
buckandbreck.com

This hidden bar – it is a dark, intimate speakeasy – is considered to be one of the best cocktail bars in the world. It was elected Bar of the Year 2015 by Mixology magazine. You have to ring the doorbell to get in, and inside there are no windows and hardly any wall-or other decoration. It's all about the awesome cocktails and the company you're in.

102 FAIRY TALE

Am Friedrichshain 24
Friedrichshain ④
+49 (0)170 2195 155
fairytale.bar

Just across from the wonderful *Märchenbrunnen* (fairy tale) fountain in the Volkspark Friedrichshain lays this hidden gem. Just ring (no sign at all) at number 24 and you might go right down the rabbit hole. Closed on Sunday and Monday. Make a reservation first, as this place gets crowded.

103 REDWOOD BAR BERLIN

Bergstrasse 25
Mitte ①
+49 (0)30 7024 8813
redwoodbar.de

This is a truly hidden gem in a quiet corner of the trendy Mitte district. The REDWOOD Bar has everything a cocktail bar needs: a bit of a mysterious exterior (look for the BAR sign in the Bergstrasse), a shabby-chic interior, a mixologist who knows exactly what you like and an eclectic crowd of friendly customers.

104 MELODY NELSON

Novalisstrasse 2
Mitte ①
+49 (0)177 7446 751

Melody Nelson opened in 2011 when this part of town was still very unhip. The neighbourhood has gone through a major transition since then, but luckily this street still isn't over-gentrified. Nothing fancy but you can count on a great atmosphere and good cocktails. Ring to get in.

105 VICTORIA BAR

Potsdamer Str. 102
Tiergarten ⑧
+49 (0)30 2575 9977
victoriabar.de

If you've ever wanted to experience the Mad Men atmosphere, this is your chance. Make sure you're dressed for success. The bar isn't really a hidden secret anymore, but it's an institution that's really worth a visit. Treat yourself to a classical concert by the amazing Berliner Philharmonic Ensemble just a block away and go for a drink in the Victoria Bar afterwards *et voilà*, there you have the perfect and classy night out.

5

HIDDEN TREASURES

---

106 **THE BLACK LODGE**
    Sanderstrasse 6
    Neukölln ⑥
    +49 (0)178 5448 099

Twin Peak fans, this one is for you. Did you know the Black Lodge really exists? Well, we're here to tell you it does. You'll find it in Kreuzberg, and it's mysterious and funky. It's also Lynchian and very affordable. But beware; this isn't a Twin Peaks theme bar. Although they do serve damn good coffee.

107 **SILENT GREEN KULTURQUARTIER**
    Gerichtstrasse 35
    Wedding ⑩
    +49 (0)30 1208 2210
    silent-green.net

A former crematorium turned into a fancy cultural hub: only in Berlin! Concerts, expositions, guided tours and a cafe and cosy restaurant called Mars that also offers an excellent, healthy lunch. We especially love the picnic concerts on the lawn in summer.

108 BAR ZENTRAL

Lotte-Lenya-Bogen 551
Charlottenburg ⑨
barzentral.de

You'll find this sophisticated bar under the train tracks, just like the Gainsbourg or The Hat Bar a little further down the road. Cognac, whisky and champagne are the main players here. Expect a cultivated public, like in many of the venues in the Savignyplatz area. Try the Tristesse Royal cocktail: we guarantee it will not make you sad.

109 ALASKA BAR

Reuterstrasse 85
Neukölln ⑥
+49 (0)30 2391 4138

Welcome to vegan Berlin in the hip district of Neukölln. Come here for after-work tapas (Andalucian style, so they're free if you buy a drink), Sunday brunch and vegan pop up events. Expect a flea market charm, cool music, cool people, lovely Spanish owners and very good prices.

110 BETH CAFÉ

Tucholskystrasse 40
Mitte ①
+49 (0)30 2813 135
adassjisroel.de/
beth-cafe

In the middle of the old Jewish quarter, just around the corner of the synagogue at the Oranienburgerstrasse lies this beautiful cafe. You can come here for hummus, falafel or *Matzeknödel* or just to enjoy a coffee in the nice backyard. Closed in the evening.

The 5 most
ECCENTRIC BARS

---

111 **BRYK**

Rykestrasse 18
Prenzlauer Berg ③
+49 (0)30 3810 0165
bryk-bar.com

Here's one of the few non-smoking bars in Berlin. It has a sunny terrace and the bar itself is a mixture of different styles: antique, design, vintage and industrial. Drinks here are among the best in the city. Bryk offers also catering, cocktail workshops, and spirits seminars.
Ring the bell or you won't get in.

112 **BAUMHAUS BAR**

Falckensteinstrasse 48
Kreuzberg ②
+49 (0)30 2391 9994

This tree house bar serves baked goods by day and booze by night. The view on the yellow U1 trains is amazing. But if you don't like it, no problem: there are a million of other bars, restaurants and clubs around the corner to choose from.

113 **WÜRGEENGEL BAR**

Dresdener Str. 122
Kreuzberg ②
+49 (0)30 6155 560
wuergeengel.de

This bar got its name from the Luis Bunuel movie *The Exterminating Angel*. In the film, the bar's visitors are caught under the angel's mysterious spell. They experience a force that doesn't allow them to move anymore. This bar aspires to have this same effect. We tried it. And it worked.

114 KLO BAR

Leibnizstrasse 57
Charlottenburg ⑨
+49 (0)30 4372 7218
(till 2 pm)
+49 (0)30 4372 7219
(after 5 pm)
klo.de

Klo means 'loo' in German; nothing more, nothing less. No kidding, the loo, that's the theme here. A very popular one apparently, and not only with students. You sit on an actual toilet while you are sipping a beer and stirring it with a small toilet brush. Really.

115 CAFÉ STRAUSS

Bergmannstrasse 42
Kreuzberg ②
+49 (0)30 6956 4453
cafestraussberlin.de

This *Friedhofcafé* (cemetery cafe) on the Friedrichwerderscher Friedhof is an oasis of serenity in hip and loud Kreuzberg. It's the perfect place for an afternoon tea or coffee (which is excellent by the way) with a long-forgotten friend.

115 CAFÉ STRAUSS

5

HIPSTER COFFEE BARS

---

116 HAPPY BARISTAS
Neue Bahnhofstr. 32
Friedrichshain ④
happybaristas.com

Right behind the Ostkreuz station lies this wonderful establishment. The wall in the back showcases artwork by street artist El Bocho. Owner Marian Plajdicko has been Slovak barista champion twice, and used to work at The Barn. Coffee (from different roasters) is taken very seriously here, and served in sea foam green cups.

117 BONANZA COFFEE ROASTERS
Oderberger Str. 35
Prenzlauer Berg ③
+49 (0)171 5630 795
bonanzacoffee.de

Passionate about coffee, like all the other roasters in Berlin, Bonanza has been setting high standards since 2006. The focus is on wholesale and consulting. Actually, no food is served here, which is really exceptional in Berlin, where everybody seems to be eating all the time. The roastery (with café) is at Adalbertstrasse 70. Their coffee is served at the Soho House Hotel – that says it all. A third location opened in the Mitte district.

118 PORTIER COFFEE

Belziger Strasse 33
Schöneberg ⑦
portiercoffee.de

The gatehouse to the former Post Office West was transformed into an elegant and cosy coffee bar at the end of 2019. It is part of the so-called Quartier Bricks Berlin, a modern ensemble of historic and newly constructed buildings between Hauptstrasse and Belziger Strasse – with flats, offices, restaurants and beautifully landscaped courtyards open to the public.

119 FATHER CARPENTER COFFEE BREWERS

Münzstrasse 21
Mitte ①
+49 (0)30 4004 4289
fathercarpenter.com

Hidden in a beautiful backyard in the busy Munzstrasse, Father Carpenter offers a nice stop for the many shoppers in this area. In summer they set up their coffee cart in the back courtyard of the 14 oz. store at Neue Schönhauser Strasse 1. There they serve coffee roasted by Fjord Coffee, the roastery they share with Silo Coffee.

120 THE BARN

Voltastrasse 28
Mitte ①
+ 9 other locations
thebarn.de

It all started in 2010 with a little Barn in the cosy Auguststrasse. By 2022, The Barn became one of the leading independent specialty coffee roasters in Europe. They have 10 locations scattered around the city. My favourite one is the cafe and roastery in Charlottenburg where The Barn took over Café Kranzler, a famous West Berlin landmark founded in 1825 that offers a panoramic view over the legendary Kurfürstendamm.

5 places with the
VERY BEST COFFEE

---

121 DOUBLEEYE
Akazienstrasse 22
Schöneberg ⑦
+49 (0)179 4566 960
doubleeye.de

European World Cup Barista champ Arno Schmeil opened DoubleEye in 2001. There are hardly any chairs, so sip your coffee standing like an Italian or join the other coffee addicts sitting in the street. This place is always (yes, always) crowded.

123 WESTBERLIN

122 FRANK CAFÉ

Schönhauser
Allee 176
Prenzlauer Berg ③
+49 (0)30 4120 7345
frankcafe.de

Probably one of the most beautiful bars in Berlin, if not the world. Restaurant & Bar KINK's little brother and neighbour has everything we love: DIY industrial furniture, five-metre-high stuccoed ceilings, plants everywhere and a fantastic garden. Add to this a great juice concept and coffee from the Berliner Kaffeerösterei and you will never want to leave this urban jungle again.

123 WESTBERLIN

Friedrichstrasse 215
Kreuzberg ②
+49 (0)30 2592 2745
westberlin-bar-shop.de

Just when you thought there is nothing near Checkpoint Charlie that is worth a visit, you stumble upon this cool coffee bar. They sell a great selection of quality magazines, they serve really good coffee and cake and they're child-, pram-, dog-, laptop-and tourist-friendly.

124 POPULUS COFFEE

Maybachufer 20
Neukölln ⑥
+49 (0)172 9884 176
populuscoffee.de

This Finnish coffee bar and roastery offers beautiful outside sitting with a view on the canal. The inside is just as nice (a good thing, because we have long winters in Berlin): very stylish, and with light colours. The coffee is self-roasted and the (mainly Nordic) treats are delicious. Try the raw citrus tartlets.

125 FIVE ELEPHANT

Reichenbergerstr. 101
Kreuzberg ②
+49 (0)30 6950 7444
fiveelephant.com

This jumbo not only serves a damn good brew but also an epic Philadelphia-style cheesecake. Five Elephant roasts its own coffee beans in the back of the shop, and yes, you probably will be tempted to buy some before your leave.

The 5 best
ALT BERLINER KNEIPEN
(old style bars)

---

126 **ZUR QUELLE**
Alt-Moabit 87
Moabit ⑨
+49 (0)30 3914 289

Open 24/24 and 365 days a year like a lot of these Alt Berliner Kneipen. Barmaid Sabine can serve 100 people all by herself and knows most of her customers by their first name. They don't make them like that anymore – that goes for the barmaid as well as for the bar.

127 **DIE HENNE BERLIN**
Leuschnerdamm 25
Kreuzberg ②
+49 (0)30 6147 730
henne-berlin.de

This bar is more than 100 years old and the same goes for the recipe for Die Henne, its legendary crispy fried chicken served with potato salad and coleslaw. Don't expect to be able to order a *chai latte* at this beautiful old-style establishment; instead they serve authentic Berlin specialties like ginger liquor, which is absolutely worth trying.

128 BESENKAMMER-BAR

Rathausstrasse 1
Mitte ①
+49 (0)30 2424 083

Located under the rails that lead to and from the Alexanderplatz station, this is one of the oldest gay bars in the city. It is open nearly 24/24 and it's very small and dark. It's also immensely popular. Despite having been a gay bar for years, they also allow women and kids – no dark rooms to be found here.

129 TIERGARTENQUELLE

Bachstrasse
S-Bahnbogen 481
and 482
Tiergarten ⑧
+49 (0)30 2472 8727
tiergartenquelle.de

Here's another establishment hidden underneath the railway. It's more a restaurant than a Kneipe but it does have that typical Kneipe atmosphere. The menu features heavy Berliner cuisine – no light salads and such. Sitting here is like going back in time, seventy years to be exact. There's a beer garden in summer.

130 DEPONIE N°3

Georgenstrasse 5
Mitte ①
+49 (0)30 2016 5740
www.deponie3.de

And yes, like the others, this Kneipe also lies under the S-Bahn tracks. 25 years ago, Russian tanks were stationed here; now it's a popular spot with students (the university is around the corner), VIPs and tourists alike. The interior is cosy and has that typical Old Berlin feeling. Nice outside terrace.

The 5 best places for
PEOPLE WATCHING

---

131 ANITA BERBER
Pankstrasse 17
Alte Fabrik Pankeweg
Wedding ⑩
+49 (0)176 6181 7262

This nightclub/art bar was named after the controversial dancer and actress Anita Berber (1899-1928). It lies hidden on the second floor of an inconspicuous building, which can only be accessed through several backyards, and it will take you straight back to the roaring twenties.

132 SCHWARZES CAFÉ
Kantstrasse 148
Charlottenburg ⑨
+49 (0)30 3138 038
schwarzescafe-berlin.de

One of the few hipster bars in Charlottenburg, with gluten-free pasta on the menu. Open 24/24 except on Tuesdays, when it's closed from 3 am till 10 am to get a good clean.

133 NEUE ODESSA BAR
Torstrasse 89
Mitte ①
neueodessabar.de

This place is open every day from 7 pm and gets full after 10 pm. Hardly any tourists come here, which for this part of town is rather unusual. The drinks are tasty and the atmosphere is seedy, but still classy, with red carpet and blurred light. No outside sitting.

134 SCHLEUSENKRUG

Müller-Breslau-
Strasse 14-B
Tiergarten ⑧
+49 (0)30 3139 909
schleusenkrug.de

This beer garden can be a little difficult to find but when you do, you won't regret it! The 'watergate pub', which is situated just behind the Zoo, in the fantastic Tiergarten, is an ideal place to rest after a stroll in the park or a visit to the Zoo. Always crowded, with both locals and tourists. You will love the Ostalgia atmosphere.

135 ROGACKI

Wilmerdorfer-
strasse 145-146
Charlottenburg ⑨
+49 (0)30 3438 250
rogacki.de

Granted, this is not exactly a hidden secret. On the contrary: Rogacki Delicatessen is almost an anachronism in this ever-changing metropolis. It started out as a smoked-fish shop in 1928. Nowadays they sell everything from champagne to cheese, meat and fish. If you're hungry, you can eat – still pretty affordably – on-site and watch life in City West go by.

133 NEUE ODESSA BAR

The 5 best
GAY BARS

---

136 CAFE NEUES UFER
　　Hauptstrasse 157
　　Schöneberg ⑦
　　+49 (0)30 7895 7900
　　neuesufer.de

Located in one of the most famous and oldest gay neighbourhoods of Berlin, this was the first gay and lesbian cafe in Europe with large street-facing windows. David Bowie and Iggy Pop lived in the house next door at the end of the 1970s and were regular guests.

140 ROSES BAR

137 SILVERFUTURE

Weserstrasse 206
Neukölln ⑥
+49 (0)30 2390 0855
silverfuture.net

A sign hanging over the bar tells patrons to leave their 'heteronormativity' at the door; if not, they can leave themselves. It's funny and it says a lot about the place, which attracts a lesbian crowd. You will love its totally chill and laidback atmosphere.

138 TOM'S BAR

Motzstrasse 19
Schöneberg ⑦
+49 (0)30 2134 570
tomsbar.de

This after hours gay bar is very popular, especially on Monday nights, when you get two drinks for the price of one. The darkroom attracts mostly fetishists and leather-clad men, who come here to cruise, so do expect a lot of action.

139 MÖBEL-OLFE

Reichenberger
Strasse 177
Kreuzberg ②
+49 (0)30 2327 4690
moebel-olfe.de

Thursday is gay night, Tuesday it's women only. And on all the other days of the week it's everything in between or behind. The building is an early 20th-century furniture (*Möbel*) house that has been turned into a lively bar, decorated by contemporary Berlin artists and designers. Go here for eclectic music and DJs and the super friendly atmosphere. The entrance is on Dresdner Strasse.

140 ROSES BAR

Oranienstrasse 187
Kreuzberg ②
+49 (0)30 6156 570

Don't let the inconspicuous outside fool you; this is a place where everything is possible. If you can't get enough of pink, plush and Virgin Mary figures, this might be your thing. It used to be a place for the LGBT crowd but that changed over the last years. Parties here go on for ever.

The 5 bars with the best
LIVE MUSIC

141 **BAR BOBU**
Schwarnweberstr. 54
Friedrichshain ②
+49 (0)30 6891 5679
barbobu.de

Easy to overlook if you miss the only sign on the street. Every Wednesday Bar Bobu has a singer-songwriter evening with sometimes surprisingly good artists on stage. It's a small place, with just a couple of chairs and tables, but it's cosy and smoky and it serves damn good Mexicano shots.

142 **PRACHTWERK**
Ganghoferstrasse 2
Neukölln ⑥
+49 (0)30 4098 563
prachtwerkberlin.com

Prachtwerk opened in 2014 and is an art gallery, a music venue and a cafe in one. It is a beautiful place with high ceilings. Coffee comes from Five Elephant roastery. All of their clear profits are invested in social projects in Berlin and all over the world.

143 **HANGAR 49**
Holzmarktstr. 15-18
Mitte ①
+49 (0)172 7443 963
hangar49.de

This music and art venue is oh so difficult to find, so be sure to follow the BVG (*Berliner Verkehrsbetriebe* – the Berlin Transport Services) footsteps. Like so many bars, it lies under the train rails but it also has a fantastic view on the Spree River. Free jam sessions every Wednesday.

144 B-FLAT

Dircksenstrasse 40
Mitte ①
+49 (0)30 2833 123
b-flat-berlin.de

B-flat is a famous jazz club in Berlin Mitte. The concept of the club: you can come here almost every night of the week and enjoy an excellent live jazz concert. Free and experimental jazz on Wednesday.

145 QUASIMODO

Kantstrasse 12-A
Charlottenburg ③
+49 (0)30 3180 4560
quasimodo.de

This is one of Berlin's oldest jazz and blues clubs. There's a jazz basement under the Delphi cinema and the Quasimodo cafe and restaurant. In summer you can have a meal or a drink on the huge patio with its Mediterranean look and feel. Prince played here in May 1987.

142 PRACHTWERK

141 BAR BOBU

5 *wonderful*
TEAROOMS

---

146 **CHÉN CHÈ TEEHAUS**
Rosenthalerstr. 13
Mitte ①
+49 (0)30 2888 4282
chenche-berlin.de

Chén Chè serves a selection of excellent Vietnamese dishes but the most important reason you should drop by, is the afternoon tea: a pot of organic green Sencha-tea and three delicacies from their family bakery, served on a wooden plate. Pay attention to their porcelain: it's just stunning.

147 **CAFÉ BUCHWALD**
Barntingallee 29
Tiergarten ⑧
+49 (0)30 3915 931
konditorei-buchwald.de

This tearoom has been in the same family for five generations now, and their speciality is *Baumkuchen* or tree cake: a kind of spit cake that gets its name from the characteristic rings that appear when it's sliced – they look like tree rings. You will also find more than 55 other cakes, pastries, and ice cakes in the bakery. It's a fantastic place for breakfast too.

148 THE COTTAGE
Blumberger Damm 44
Marzahn
+49 (0)30 9599 86338
thecottageberlin.de

A little off the beaten track but too good not to mention and very close to Gärten der Welt. Proof that Berlin has it all! Do you have a hankering for some tea and homemade cake and a rose garden? Look no further. This tiny English cottage serves one of the best high teas in town. Utterly British, indeed.

149 CAFÉ SIBYLLE
Karl-Marx-Allee 72
Friedrichshain ④
+49 (0)30 2935 2203
café-sibylle.de

The big Karl Marx Allee used to be called the Stalin Allee and it has a very interesting past. In Café Sibylle there's a permanent exposition of old photographs of this avenue. They also sometimes organise tours here (only in German). Have some coffee and cake and enjoy a perfect afternoon at a historical location.

150 TADSHIKISCHE TEESTUBE
Oranienburger Str. 27
Mitte ①
+49 (0)30 2041 112
tadshikische-teestube.de

The whole interior of this splendid teahouse was a gift from the former Soviet constituent republic Tajikistan to the GDR. The venue opened in 1976 but has moved since then. The tea is served in original *samovars* – a Russian metal container that's used to make tea. The *samovar* tea ceremonies are very popular so please book well in advance.

The 5 best
BARS FOR SINGLES

---

151 CLÄRCHENS BALLHAUS
Auguststrasse 24
Mitte ①
+49 (0)30 2829 295
claerchensball.haus

Clärchens is an institution, nothing more, nothing less. Whether you have a meal in the garden of this old ballroom or sit inside, you will enjoy watching the scenes. There are special so-called Schwoof nights for singles on Friday and Saturday. Locals as well as tourists love it here. Same owners as the legendary Strandbar Mitte.

152 FISCH SUCHT FAHRRAD
AT: FRANNZ CLUB
(KULTURBRAUEREI)
Schönhauser Allee 36
Prenzlauer Berg ③
+49 (0)30 8485 0923
fischsucht fahrrad.berlin

Fisch sucht Fahrrad (which means 'fish looking for a bike') is probably the most popular party night for singles in Berlin. Every two weeks it takes place in the Frannz Club in the beautiful Kulturbrauerei. Try your best German on a speed dating night, and maybe you'll find the love of your life. Whether you are the fish or the bike doesn't really matter.

153 BALLHAUS BERLIN

Chausseestrasse 102
Mitte ①
+49 (0)30 2827 575
ballhaus-berlin.de

Forget Whatsapp and Tinder and bring back those numbered *Tischtelefonen* (table phones) on nightclub tables, enabling smooth calls to whoever catches your eye. These were once *en vogue* in most of Berlin's Weimar-era clubs and ballrooms, and they're still there in the Ballhaus Berlin as a unique survivor of the city's racy pre-war heyday. Get ready to flirt, retro-style.

154 DSCHUNGEL

Friedelstrasse 12
Neukölln ⑥

This bar, restaurant, cinema, coffee bar and what else is not exactly for singles only but you can spend the whole night here watching movies or people while enjoying a coffee or a beer. The walls are all covered with jungle-patterned wallpaper. Me Tarzan, you Jane?

155 8MM BAR

Schonhauser
Allee 177-B
Prenzlauer Berg ③
+49 (0)30 4050 0624
8mmbar.de

One of the few rock 'n roll bars in a techno obsessed city. Prenzlauer Berg, now the most gentrified of all hoods in Berlin, used to be the place to be for artists and anarchists of all kinds. This venue, which has its own distillery where they make gin, absinthe and bitters, still reflects that vibe.

5 bars with an
AMAZING VIEW

---

156 KLUNKERKRANICH
AT: NEUKÖLLN ARCADEN
Karl-Marx-Strasse 66
Neukölln ① ⑥
klunkerkranich.de

The leafy roof of the ugly Neukölln Arcaden shopping centre is where the Neukölln hipsters and young families come together to listen to DJs playing tunes and to watch the sun set over the rooftops of Berlin. Fusion cuisine, flea markets, cocktail bars and much more, all on (not under) one roof. Only in summer, of course.

157 DECK5
Rooftop Schön-
hauser Arcaden
Prenzlauer Berg ③
+49 (0)30 4172 8905
deck-5.com/de

Deck5 is a beach bar on the 7th floor of a car park and it's the first and the highest 'skybeach' in Berlin offering 400 m² of beach fun, 63 metres above sea level. Chill on a couch, sip a cocktail and admire the TV-tower, Berlin's highest landmark, while your naked toes are drawing circles in the white sand.

158 MONBIJOU HOTEL
Monbijouplatz 1
Mitte ①
+49 (0)30 6162 0300
monbijouhotel.com

This cosy rooftop terrace of a relatively small boutique hotel is a real hidden gem: it offers incredible 360-degree views of Berlin. You can see the Dome and the Museum Island, the Radio Tower, the entire Scheunenviertel and the Hackescher Markt.

159 **ANDEL'S HOTEL SKYKITCHEN**
Landsberger Allee 106
Lichtenberg
+49 (0)30 4530 53 2620
skykitchen.berlin

A little bit further away from the hip city centre, in an area that's often overlooked by glossy magazines and other so-called trendsetters, you'll find this pretty new hotel. It boasts two hidden gems on the 14th floor: one is a Michelin-starred restaurant called the Skykitchen, the other is the Skybar, where you can have excellent drinks while enjoying a fantastic view on the city.

160 **HOUSE OF WEEKEND**
Alexanderstrasse 7
Mitte ①
+49 (0)152 2429 3140
houseofweekend.berlin

This Club is located in a building on Alexanderplatz called the Haus des Reisens. The House of Weekend occupies the 12th, 15th and rooftop terrace floors of this old Soviet tower block, offering its visitors an absolutely fantastic view on Alexanderplatz and its surroundings. In summer it opens every day at 7 pm.

156 KLUNKERKRANICH

The 5 best
WINE BARS

---

161 **OTTORINK**
   Dresdenerstr. 124
   Kreuzberg ②
   +49 (0)30 6098 09270
   ottorink.de

This charming and cosy wine bar was named after the current owner's grandfather, and it's the oldest wine bar in town, with a focus on wines made in Germany. Owner Andreas is also a trained winemaker, and he has a soft spot for the Mosel wines. There's a giant blackboard in the bar, with a huge list of wines that can be ordered by the glass.

162 **LUST BAR**
   Torstrasse 225
   Mitte ①
   +49 (0)170 8813 088
   lust-bar.com

Only French wines in the Lust bar (which is a fantastic name for a bar, by the way). You can also get some cheese and sausages plates with different tapenades to go along. Lunch is really fairly priced. Owner Romuald often organises events or pop ups in his bar. Check the website.

163 JAJA

Weichselstrasse 7
Neukölln ⑥
+49 (0)30 5266 6911
jajawein.de

One of the most laidback wine bars in town. Owners Julia and Etienne present a collection of natural wines, with an emphasis on France. Natural wines are wines made with minimal chemical and technological intervention.Chef Yailen Diaz cooks up an excellent weekly menu that is in line with their selection of wines.

164 HAMMERS WEINKOSTBAR

Körtestrasse 20
Kreuzberg ②
+49 (0)30 6981 8677
hammers-wein.de

Sommelier Jürgen Hammer and his partner Manuela Sporbert are the driving forces behind this very down-to-earth and cosy wine bar. The place used to be a *Fleischerei* (butcher's shop) and some of the old interior elements are still there, for a unique vintage feel. Come here for the excellent advice on wine and for the carefully chosen (mostly French) cheeses and paté.

165 GALLINA-VINERIA BAR

Pücklerstrasse 20
Kreuzberg ②
+49 (0)30 4176 6550
bargallina.de

Same owners as Der Goldener Hahn and Fratelli la Bionda. All three restaurants serve really good Italian food in a cosy and typical Italian atmosphere. The Gallina is the one that is specialised in antipasti and wine. Most of the wines are imported from Italy from small independent wine growers.

The 5 best bars
TO GET SOME WORK DONE

---

166 **SANKT OBERHOLZ**
Rosenthaler Str. 72-A
Mitte ①
+49 (0)30 5557 8595
sanktoberholz.de

When you think of the Rosenthaler Platz, you think of its cars, its bikes, its döner kebab shops and its hipsters. But also of its Sankt Oberholz, where you can find co-working spaces, conference rooms, a nice and big bar, and even apartments. The food and the drinks are excellent and the atmosphere is pleasant, but the chances you will be sitting in front of a MacBook instead of a real person are pretty high.

167 **DISTRIKT COFFEE**
Bergstrasse 68
Mitte ①
distriktcoffee.de

Another excellent and tastefully designed coffee bar situated in a peaceful, not yet totally gentrified street. Please note that the coffee is strong: all drinks are served with double shots which is of course a perfect way to start a day of hard work, especially if you combine it with one of their really excellent breakfasts.

168 GODSHOT

Immanuelkirchstr. 32
Prenzlauer Berg ③
+49 (0)179 5112 643
godshot.de

Apart from being an excellent coffee bar (with a nice and sunny terrace), you can also come here for workshops and seminars. The passion of the baristas for their coffee is nearly palpable and service is very friendly. Young children are also welcome – hence the toys that are at their disposal in the downstairs room. There are some very interesting shops in the neighbourhood.

169 CAFÉ BILDERBUCH

Akazienstrasse 28
Schöneberg ⑦
+49 (0)30 7870 6057
cafe-bilderbuch.de

Gallery, library, bar, restaurant: this venue has many different faces. It has several rooms and an outdoor courtyard as well as a front terrace. There's a piano in the backroom and sometimes somebody is bold enough to play it. It's a truly pleasant place that looks like it's been around for ages. They serve brunch too.

170 KLEINMEIN

Waldeyerstrasse 9
Friedrichshain ④
+49 (0)177 5603 701
kleinmein.gr

This small and exceptionally beautiful cafe has a separate co-working room and has not yet been overtaken by hipsters. They offer flexible hourly tickets that come with a free hot beverage. Open every day from 11 am to 5 pm.

The 5
HEALTHIEST BARS

---

171 **ELEMENT 5**
Skalitzer Strasse 46-B
Kreuzberg ②
+49 (0)30 7732 1152
element-five.de

Element 5 serves delicious vegan Cantonese tapas in a very beautiful *altbau* corner house. Healthy fresh food to share with friends before diving into Kreuzbergs sizzling nightlife, what's not to like? Tip: three tapas per person are more than enough and make sure to order the Peking Duck!

172 **DALUMA**
Weinbergsweg 3
Mitte ①
+49 (0)30 2095 0255
daluma.de

Daluma almost immediately won the hearts of the hip Mitte crowd with its cold juices, smoothies and a few health shots. They also serve tasty raw, vegan food. Seating is limited so have your order to go and enjoy it in the Weinbergpark, like so many others do.

173 FUNK YOU NATURAL FOOD

Rosenthaler Str. 23
Mitte ①
+49 (0)176 6105 5335
*funkyou
naturalfood.com*

Tired of shopping in this fancy area, crammed with shops and bars? Go and have a coffee or lunch at Funk You and watch the hipsters go by through the big window. This place specialises in raw food, smoothies and has a decent range of vegan food including cakes, sandwiches and soups.

174 GOODIES

Warschauerstr. 69
Friedrichshain ④
+49 (0)30 4403 6048
goodies-berlin.de

Goodies is a vegetarian and vegan deli with several outlets. The salads are especially tasty but the sweet stuff like the strawberry almond tarte or the power chia pudding is irresistible as well. And the coffee is simply delicious.

175 BJUICE

Metzerstrasse 10
Prenzlauer Berg ③
+49 (0)30 4005 3400
bjuice.de

Beshar and Susi studied in California, and that's where they learned all about how to nurture a healthy mind in a healthy body. Back home in Germany, they decided to open a cold pressed raw juice bar. They also offer 1 day, 3 day or 5 day juice detox packages. We particularly like the small health shots.

The 5 coolest
BEER GARDENS
and/or BREWERIES

---

176 **ESCHENBRAÜ**
Triftstrasse 67
Wedding ⑩
+49 (0)162 4931 915
eschenbraeu.de

Eschenbraü is located in the cellar of an apartment complex in Wedding. It's a mix of brewery and beer garden. The cellar spills out into a fun courtyard. Here you can get either one of the three traditional brews *(pilsner, dunkel* or *hefeweizen)* or one of the nine seasonal brews. It's really a beer lover biergarten. And absolutely worth a visit.

177 **BIERHOF RÜDERSDORF**
Rüdersdorfer Str. 70
Friedrichshain ④
+49 (0)30 2936 0215
www.bierhof.info

This peaceful spot is located behind the techno temple called Berghain. It's fun to have breakfast in the sun here and look at those tired faces when they're coming out of this legendary club after 48 or maybe even more hours of partying.

178 ZOLLPACKHOF

Elisabeth-Abegg-
Strasse 1
Mitte ①
+49 (0)30 3309 970
zollpackhof.de

A little more posh than most beer gardens, maybe because of its location in the Regierungsviertel close to the Reichstag and other government buildings. On the menu there are some excellent German dishes with Mediterranean twists. In winter, there's a nice fireplace.

179 VAGABUND

Antwerpener Str. 3
Wedding ⑩
+49 (0)30 5266 7668
vagabundbrauerei.com

Three Americans in Berlin; it could have been the title of a movie but it's the background story of this brewery, founded by a trio from the US in the former French district of Berlin. They brew six different beers, including a triple beer for which they use a very special Belgian yeast. You can taste their craft beer on tap in their beautiful taproom and you can visit the brewery. Or you can even take some brewery courses.

180 HOPFENREICH

Sorauer Strasse 31
Kreuzberg ②
+49 (0)30 8806 1080
hopfenreich.de

This bar has no less than 22 beers on tap. The people behind the bar renovated an old *Ecke Kneipe* (corner bar) and raised beer tasting to a higher level. Try the local brews and take a look at the beautiful steampunky bar. They also organise Berlin Craft Beer Tours and tastings.

BADESCHIFF

30 PLACES
TO GO OUT

---

5 *extraordinary*
DANCE VENUES

---

181 UFERSTUDIOS

Badstrasse 41-A
Mitte ①
+49 (0)30 4606 0887
uferstudios.com

From an electrical trolley depot to studios for contemporary dance, this historically protected area that houses Uferstudios is well worth a visit. Take a peek in their garden, grab lunch at Lokarasa on-site and have a coffee in a reconverted bus at Pförtners in the Uferstrasse before you go for a walk along the Panke rivulet for a perfect day.

182 BEBOP

Pfuelstrasse 5
Friedrichshain ④
+49 (0)176 3149 0257
bebop-berlin.com

Bebop is located on the ground floor of a former warehouse that was constructed in 1908. This beautiful venue organises a so-called 'Tango Café' every Saturday afternoon and a 'Tango Bar' every Tuesday evening. Stand or dance on the big terrace with a view on the TV tower and the East Side Gallery, with the water of the Spree-river reflecting in the evening sun: it's a priceless experience.

183 DAS WALZERLINKS-GESTRICKT

Am Tempelhofer
Berg 7-D
Kreuzberg ②
+49 (0)30 6950 5000
walzerlinksgestrickt.de

This *Ballhaus* focuses mainly on tango but you can also take salsa and swing classes. The ballroom, with its 6,6-metre-high ceiling, its gallery and its red velvet curtains, reflects the culture of Berlin in the 20s and 30s. Saturday is their biggest *milonga* (tango evening). It's hosted by DJ Michael Rühl, who's also the organiser of the Tango Festival Berlin.

184 DOCK 11

Kastanienallee 79
Prenzlauer Berg ③
+49 (0)30 4481 222
dock11-berlin.de

Prenzlauer Berg might be an area (or *Kiez*) where the gentrification of Berlin is very palpable, but there are still places with a very strong Ostalgia vibe. DOCK 11 is one of those places. Situated in a typical *Mietskaserne* backyard, it is a beautiful venue for dance and theatre. Few but very good live events.

185 INSOMNIA

Alt Tempelhof 17-19
Alt Tempelhof
+49 (0)177 2333 878
insomnia-berlin.de

Insomnia is an erotic nightclub that organises all kinds of (very!) kinky parties. Every second Wednesday of the month you can go to a 'Tango Vicioso' night at the ballroom on the first floor. The room has a wonderful fin de siècle feeling to it and the music – a mix of old and new tango – is simply fantastic. A word of advice: you better be open-minded and dressed for the occasion.

The 5 most
TRENDY CLUBS

---

186 PRINCE CHARLES

Prinzenstrasse 85-F
(Moritzplatz)
Kreuzberg ②
*princecharles
berlin.com*

Prince Charles resides in a large, re-designed space and that's what distinguishes this club from most of the other, grungier clubs in the city. The sunken-level bar is cool and slick. The drinks here might be a little more expensive than in other bars, but don't let this keep you from drinking a delicious Lady Diana cocktail. The programming is eclectic, with a focus on electronic music.

187 SALON ZUR WILDEN RENATE

Alt-Stralau 70
Friedrichshain ④
+49 (0)30 2504 1426
renate.cc

Salon zur Wilden Renate is a typical Berliner multi-floor and multi-room house-club par excellence. Clubbers as well as staff are all nice and friendly here, and a bit weird too – as you can expect in the coolest Berlin venues. The atmosphere is very theatrical and there's also a fabulous outdoor courtyard; it's open in summer, but sometimes also in winter.

188 KATER BLAU

Holzmarktstrasse 25
Mitte ①
+49 (0)30 5105 2134
katerblau.de

This legendary club had to move in 2014 because of the gentrification of its former neighbourhood. But the fans had nothing to worry about: the atmosphere stayed the same. There's a lot of outdoor space, there are several dance floors and chill out areas, food and drinks are cheap, the electro music is excellent and the new location close to the Spree is really nice; this club is a worthy Hidden Secret.

189 KITKATCLUB

Köpenicker Str. 76
Mitte ①
kitkatclub.org

KitKat is more than a club; it's a place for hedonists. A place where love and lust are taken to a higher level, and where they're taken seriously and with respect for everyone's desires. So if you decide to go clubbing in the KitKat: be prepared to have a grand night out where everything is possible. Meouaw.

190 ://ABOUT BLANK

Markgrafen-
damm 24-C
Friedrichshain ④
aboutblank.li

This used to be an illegal club. Now the interior of this repurposed building has been slightly renovated. It features seemingly endless nooks and crannies and two main dancefloors inside. During summer DJs and sometimes bands perform in the playful garden, which is open in winter too, often with a bonfire going. Awesome sound system.

5 bars or mini-clubs where
DANCING IS PERMITTED

---

191 BADESCHIFF

Eichenstrasse 4
Friedrichshain ④
+49 (0)30 5332 030
*arena.berlin/
veranstaltungsort/
badeschiff*

Have a container floating on the river, fill it with water and there you go: you've got THE perfect swimming pool. The view on the Media Spree, the Oberbaumbrücke and the monumental Molecule Man sculpture is priceless.

192 DAS HOTEL (CLUB)

Mariannenstrasse 26
Kreuzberg ②
+49 (0)30 8411 8433
dashotel.org

Much more than a hotel: this is also a bar, a restaurant (The Bistro) and a club. Rooms can only be booked by e-mail. Das Hotel tries to be a counterforce against all the commercialism that nowadays is typical of this kind of venues and hipster districts.

193 ALTER ROTER LÖWE REIN

Richardstrasse 31
Neukölln ⑥
+49 (0)151 2068 8670

A typical Berlin *Wohnzimmer Bar* (living room bar) with an international clientele, as is often the case in this lovely Rixdorf *Kiez*. But this is more than just a bar: the middle room is used for live concerts as well as tango dancing and stand-up comedy. Add in the nice atmosphere and some Bavarian beer and the evening can't go wrong.

194 OH! CALCUTTA

Koloniestrasse 9
Wedding ⑩
+49 (0)176 7677 6842
ohcalcutta-bar.de

Oh! Calcutta is a funky, elegant cocktail bar that also organises concerts and jam sessions. The fact that this venue lies off the beaten track is a huge advantage: it's not too crowded like bars in other districts often are.

195 BAR TAUSEND

Schiffbauerdamm 11
Mitte ①
+49 (0)30 2758 2070
tausendberlin.com

This fancy club, bar and Asian & Ibero-American restaurant is pretty difficult to find. Look for the stark iron door shadowed by the Paris-Moskau railway. The bar is enormous and the 'Moscow Mule' cocktail legendary. Better make a reservation if you want to eat at the restaurant.

194 OH! CALCUTTA

5 places to enjoy a good
CABARET or
BURLESQUE SHOW

---

196 WINTERGARTEN

Potsdamer Str. 96
Tiergarten ⑧
+49 (0)30 588 433
wintergarten-berlin.de

Not exactly a hidden secret now that this area is upcoming; namely lots of very good art galleries are emerging here. Wintergarten itself is one of the most beautiful variety theatres in Europe. Think mirrors, wood, a starry sky and dark red velvet and you'll get an idea of the atmosphere. It's the place to go for (often large-scale) burlesque, cabaret, and live music shows.

197 PRINZIPAL

Oranienstrasse 178
Kreuzberg ②
+49 (0)30 6162 7326
prinzipal-kreuzberg.com

Prinzipal has nothing to do with the *Wohnzimmer* (living room) feeling that's so typical for venues in Berlin. On the contrary; it has a distinct jazzy and nostalgic vibe. It's cosy and small, and ideal for after dinner drinks. On Saturday they often program burlesque shows.

198 KLEINE NACHTREVUE

Kurfürstenstrasse 116
Schöneberg ⑧
+49 (0)30 2188 950
kleine-nachtrevue.de

On the Kurfürstenstrasse you'll see streethookers trying to score (remember Christiane F?) but also the famous French college where well-educated children are raised. This is also where you will find this nightclub: a classy erotic theatre with a hedonistic 1920s atmosphere and a touch of avant-garde.

199 ZUM STARKEN AUGUST

Schönhauser Allee 56
Prenzlauer Berg ③
+49 (0)30 2520 9020
zumstarkenaugust.de

Great entertainment and lots of nice burlesque shows take place in this cosy and nicely decorated bar. They also serve a great selection of craft beers and breakfast on Sundays. Sensible prices. Check their website to see who's performing.

200 VAUDEVILLE VARIETY BURLESQUE REVUE

VARIOUS LOCATIONS
vaudeville-variety.com

This burlesque festival takes place yearly in September, at Tipi am Kanzleramt or at the Admiralspalast. Expect the best of both the Berlin and the international burlesque scene, but also kinky boylesque, freak shows, striptease, and cabaret. Book your ticket online.

5 totally
DIFFERENT
ways to party

---

201 CLUB KAFFEE BURGER

Torstrasse 60
Mitte ①
+49 (0)30 2804 6495
kaffeeburger.de

This sweaty cult club has a very eclectic sound policy and organises lots of readings and/or poetry slams. The Kaffee is especially well known for its Russen-disko (*www.russendisko.de*) evenings, an initiative of writer Wladimir Kaminer, who wrote a book with the same title and who regularly DJs on those nights.

202 CAKE CLUB

Mariannenstrasse 27
Kreuzberg ②
+49 (0)151 4702 4310

Cake Club is a tiny, cosy nightclub in the buzzing Kreuzberg district. You have to pay a small cover charge and then you're in for a night of rock music, Balkan beats and independent music – and that's rather exceptional in Berlin, a city that has embraced electronic music.

203 SAMEHEADS

Richardstrasse 10
Neukölln ⑥
+49 (0)30 7012 1060
sameheads.com

There used to be a time when Neukölln was considered a no-go area in Berlin. It was seen as dirty and dangerous. Now it attracts hipsters from all over the world. Sameheads, a small club where literally everything is possible and nothing is too weird, reflects this international scene very well. Come early, it gets full very quick.

204 CLUB DER VISIONAERE

Am Flutgraben 1
Treptow ⑤
+49 (0)30 6951 8942
clubdervisionaere.com

This tiny club is housed in a small brick building on the bank of a canal, with offices upstairs and a dancefloor downstairs. The weeping willow that hangs over a part of the club is particularly charming; in summer most of the people will hang out here. In 2016 the Club decided to charter the Hoppetosse boat; it functions as the new sun deck and an extra winter indoor location.

205 ANOMALIE ART CLUB

Storkower Strasse 123
Prenzlauer Berg ③

More than a club, Anomalie is an art centre. An open, creative, and exhilaratingly visionary space presented by Stay Free Kollektiv, who state that their project is not driven by money – which explains why they don't feel the need to follow any trends. Expect to meet some VERY open-minded people.

The 5 best
KARAOKE VENUES

---

206 GREEN MANGO

Bülowstrasse 56-57
Kreuzberg ②
+49 (0)30 7563 7394
greenmango24.de

This is Europe's biggest karaoke venue, offering nearly 700 m² of karaoke fun with lots of German music. There's a lounge bar and a restaurant. The place is very loud and very young and very popular. Only for die-hard karaoke fans!

207 MONSTER RONSON'S ICHIBAN KARAOKE

Warschauerstrasse 34
Friedrichshain ③
+49 (0)30 8975 1327
karaokemonster.de

If you thought karaoke was boring you should definitely try Monster Ronson; it's the trendiest karaoke bar in town, with the most international vibe. It's super popular so you have to make a reservation a couple of days (or sometimes even weeks) beforehand. There are different private booths.

208 HAFENBAR BERLIN

Karl-Liebknecht-Str. 11
Mitte ①
+49 (0)30 2828 593
hafenbar-berlin.de

This bar in former East Berlin has been around for about five decades and all this time it has been conducted by the same man, Captain Klaus Zagermann. Western journalists weren't allowed in until after 1974 when you could buy a pass to go from West to East Berlin. This bar is probably responsible for bringing the so-called Balkan beats to the West.

209 BEARPIT KARAOKE

Mauerpark
Prenzlauer Berg ③
+49 (0)157 8065 6279
bearpitkaraoke.com

A summer Sunday afternoon at the flea market at the Mauerpark just isn't the same when you don't attend the legendary Bearpit Karaoke. The stone amphitheatre will be crowded with good nurtured people who sing along with the karaoke singer in the middle. Joe Hatchiban uses portable, battery-powered boxes to help people unleash their inner Bianca Castafiore.

210 NOKA KOREA KARAOKE

Schulstrasse 29
Wedding ⑩
+49 (0)30 6174 6796

If you've always wanted to sing in Korean, Japanese, Mongolian or whatever other foreign language you might think of: this is the place to be. There's a typically Asian, kitschy ambiance and you can enjoy Korean cuisine. You will definitely forget you're actually in Berlin. For a special night out.

TYPE HYPE

80 PLACES TO SHOP TILL YOU DROP

The 5 best shops for
BERLIN FASHION

211 STOKX SHOP+STUDIO
Steinstrasse 26
Mitte ①
+49 (0)30 2804 5268
stokx.de

Stokx used to be situated in the famous Schwarzenberg house, but moved to the more artsy Steinstrasse. We were very much enchanted by this label: Stokx is known for its beautiful but highly wearable pieces, all made in Berlin. No flashy colours, no snobbery and exquisite quality: what's not to love?

212 LALA BERLIN
Alte Schönhauser
Strasse 3
Mitte ①
+49 (0)30 2009 5363
lalaberlin.com

Leyla Piedayesh (who was born in Teheran) started selling her hand-knit pieces on the flea market. Now, her unconventional, elegant and often colourful designs have conquered the world. Cameron Diaz, Jessica Alba and Natalie Portman are big fans.

213 KONK/MITTE
Kleine Hamburger
Strasse 15
Mitte ①
+49 (0)30 2809 7839
konk-berlin.de

Konk is a very small shop in one of the cutest streets of Berlin, specialised in Berlin based designers and labels. The very helpful and passionate shop-keeper Edda Mann is always looking for new talent.

214 THONE NEGRÓN

Linienstrasse 71
Mitte ①
+49 (0)30 5316 1116
thonenegron.com

Thone Negrón was founded by (former Konk owner) Ettina Berrios-Negron in 2008. It's best known for its fabulous wedding dresses but the label also offers ready-to-wear pieces and exclusive dresses. The design is classic but at the same time the clothes look very contemporary.

215 MOON BERLIN

Erich-Weinert-Str. 15
Prenzlauer Berg ③
+49 (0)30 4195 7796
moonberlin.com

It's not every day that you find a fashion label that cooperates with nasa, yet that's what Moon Berlin is. The label was founded by Christian Bruns in 2010, when he started to research the innovative production processes of the future. The radically modern label now stands for unique designs and long-lasting quality. Try on one of their heated cashmere coats.

The 5 most unique
CONCEPT STORES

216 THE CORNER

Französische Str. 40
Mitte ①
+49 (0)30 2067 0940
thecornerberlin.de

Tired of Berlin's shabby chic and in the mood to really dress up like a film star? Then this is the place you should go to. In this huge (750 m²) concept store on the very touristy but oh so beautiful Gendarmenmarkt, you'll find international luxury fashion brands like Louboutin or Hermès but also design furniture, perfumes and jewellery. There's also a Corner in Charlottenburg and a smaller one in Mitte.

217 SOUL OBJECTS

Prenzlauer Allee 24
Prenzlauer Berg ③
+49 (0)30 6800 6076
soulobjects.de

Every time I pass by this store, I can't help but stare at the ever-changing and often mesmerising objects in the window. Not everything is vintage, but you can expect to find carefully curated objects like traditional grooming and shaving tools, porcelain plates with tattoo motifs or exclusive perfumes just to name a few. If you're looking for a special present, you definitely came to the right place.

220 **TYPE HYPE**

218 ANDREAS MURKUDIS

Potsdamer Str. 81-E
Tiergarten ⑧
+49 (0)30 6807 98306
andreasmurkudis.com

Andreas Murkudis used to be the director of the design museum in Berlin. His knack for beauty and aesthetics is palpable in all of his stores. He only sells products he would love to own himself because of their exceptional design. With two stores in the Potsdamer Strasse and one in the fabulous Bikini Haus (the world's first concept shopping mall), Murkudis is here to stay.

219 VOOSTORE

Oranienstrasse 24
Kreuzberg ②
+49 (0)30 9120 6690
vooberlin.com

Hipster alert! Here are 300 m² filled with the collections of hip and upscale brands (Joseph, Acné Studios, Alexander Wang...) on the premises of a former locksmith shop in a backyard on the Oranienstrasse. The in-store coffee shop serves absolutely delicious coffee and cakes.

220 TYPE HYPE

Rosa-Luxemburg-
Strasse 9-13
Mitte ①
+49 (0)30 3027 5914
typehype.com

Small is beautiful. At least here it is. TYPE HYPE offers a wonderful selection of premium designer products (cups, cushions, stationary...) all featuring the letters of the alphabet. The label stands for sustainable, handmade and local (in Berlin) manufacturing but also for metropolitan, hip and stylish designs. On top of that they serve very good coffee and breakfast from 8 am till 8 pm.

The 5 most charming
VINTAGE SHOPS

221 VINTAGE LIVING
Oranienstrasse 53
Kreuzberg ②
+49 (0)30 6959 9496
vintageliving.de

This very big vintage shop focuses on design classics from the twentieth century. Don't expect to find a bargain here, but do know that all lamps, furniture and accessories are original.

222 OBJETS TROUVÉS
Brunnenstrasse 169
Mitte ①
+49 (0)151 7250 4383
objets-trouves-berlin.de

Magdalena and Robert have a beautiful selection of carefully restored antique furniture, but they specialise in tables. All of these tables are customised and completely handmade from sustainable materials like glass, steel, wood or stone.

223 CHAIRS
Fehrbelliner Str. 25
Prenzlauer Berg ③
+49 (0)30 4435 5723
shop.chairs-design.com

Whether it's the famous black leather armchair by Eames, the functional pieces by Mies van der Rohe or the orange Egg by Arne Jacobsen, chances are you will find one of those iconic chairs here, next to a few lamps, couches and tables. The shop on the beautiful Zionskirchplatz is bright and a little bit chaotic. It's only open in the afternoon.

224 J&V FINEST INDUSTRIAL VINTAGE FURNITURE

Barbarossastrasse 61
Schöneberg ⑦
+49 (0)163 2907 831
jandv.eu

Jools and Vince sell industrial furniture exclusively; so don't expect the great design classics here – although the French Jielde lamps might be considered as such. The owners share a love of artefacts from the former GDR, which have a certain charm about them, being witnesses of a very specific time in history.

225 ORIGINAL IN BERLIN

Karl-Marx-Allee 83
Friedrichshain ④
+49 (0)30 6093 6046
originalinberlin.com

500 m² filled with mid-century design furniture and located in a fantastic building on the impressive Karl Marx Allee: what's not to love? This Berlin showroom not only features the iconic vintage pieces but also a nice collection of contemporary accessories designed by Carl Auböck.

5 original
MADE IN BERLIN
brands

---

226 SCHOEMIG PORZELLAN

Raumerstrasse 35
Prenzlauer Berg ③
+49 (0)30 6954 5513
schoemig-porzellan.de

Claudia Schoemig had won tens of prices with her fine paper-like porcelain pieces before she decided to open her shop. Everything here is made the old-school way, so without any help of moulds. Most of the pieces are translucent which makes them look oh so vulnerable but don't worry: because of porcelain's hardness all the bowls, cups and vases are fit to be used in daily life.

227 LIEBESKIND BERLIN

Neue Schönhauser
Strasse 8
Mitte ①
+49 (0)30 2478 1600
de.liebeskind-berlin.com

In my opinion, one of the most beautiful brand names in the world: *Liebeskind* actually means Lovechild. Berlin is indeed home, location AND muse of this bag-, shoes- and accessories manufacturer and that since 2003. Liebeskind Berlin is now one of the biggest German fashion labels and their bags are recognisable by their cool, functional vintage look.

228 CREATORS BERLIN

Karl-Marx-Strasse 26
Neukölln ⑥
creatorsberlin.com

Joseph Marr (born in Australia) and Sansara Van (born in Mongolia), both very much influenced by the city's techno scene, make very distinctive street art sculptures. A nine-metre-long sugar work by Joseph's hand can even be seen in the über techno temple Berghain. Sansara on her side often works for the five opera houses in Berlin. Together they produce rather cute small sculptures for a larger public.

229 STANDERT BICYCLES

Invalidenstrasse 157
Mitte ①
+49 (0)30 2844 4219
standert.de

Berlin loves bikers and – as a logical consequence – bikes. Standert is not only a bike shop but also, and above all, a brand of bicycles made primarily out of steel. Because this is Berlin, the shop also features a cafe space. The Dutch cycling magazine Soigneur named Standert one of the 25 best cycling shops in the world.

230 FRAU TONIS PARFUM

Zimmerstrasse 13
Kreuzberg ②
+49 (0)30 2021 5310
frau-tonis-parfum.com

You wouldn't think of Berlin as a city of perfume manufacturers but it turns out there are quite a few. The Different Scent in the Krausnickstrasse for example focuses on rare and original small brands. Frau Tonis is more of a niche perfumery house. All the perfumes here are made from high quality essential oils from France. The founder of the house is Stefanie Hanssen, the granddaughter of Toni Gronewald, who was known as 'Frau Toni'.

The 5 coolest
VINYL STORES

231 MELTING POINT RECORD STORE

Kastanienallee 55
Prenzlauer Berg ③
+49 (0)30 4404 7131

The interior of this shop is very basic but that's okay because music is what's it all about, more specifically house, disco and boogie. Fans of those genres will be able to spend hours here, digging for the perfect record.

232 33RPM STORE

Wrangelstrasse 95
Kreuzberg ②
33rpmstore.com

33rpm store is a small but truly nice shop inside the cafe Mukkefukk in the Kreuzberg district. Here you'll find both second-hand and new records, but the store specialises in used vinyl records for collectors. They also regularly host live concerts here.

233 OYE RECORDS

Oderbergerstrasse 4
Prenzlauer Berg ③
+49 (0)30 6664 7821
oye-records.com

One of the biggest vinyl stores in town with an incredibly varied music selection. They often host in-store sessions: a mix of live performances and DJ sets that never disappoint. Entry is free.

234 VINYL-A-GOGO

Krossener Strasse 24
Friedrichshain ④
+49 (0)174 1749 999
vinyl-a-gogo.com

One of the nicest shops around Boxhagener Platz. The service is friendly and the selection is eclectic with a focus on reggae and hiphop. You can also find a lot of obscure German krautrock if that's what you're looking for. The interior is anything but fancy but the records are very well sorted.

235 AUDIO-IN USED RECORD STORE

Libauerstrasse 19
Friedrichshain ④
+49 (0)30 4862 2984
audio-in.net

Located near the famous techno temple Berghain, this is the place to be if you're looking for used drum-'n-bass records, house, electro, techno and even Italo disco. Owner Martin Rieser used to sell vinyl on the flea markets for years; now the shelves in his shop carry over 5000 titles. Decent prices and clean records.

5 *wonderful*

INDEPENDENT BOOKSTORES

---

236 OCELOT

Brunnenstrasse 181
Mitte ①
+49 (0)30 9789 4592
ocelot.de

This beautiful, oak panelled bookstore is connected with the library of Berlin's Mitte-district. There's a carefully curated selection of fiction and non-fiction, children's books, and arty magazines. The English selection is small but you won't mind when you know there's an in-store coffee bar where it's totally okay to sip coffee and eat cake (made by Wunderkuchen) while reading.

237 ZABRISKIE

Reichenberger-
strasse 150
Kreuzberg ②
+49 (0)30 6956 6714
zabriskie.de

This super cute and charming bookstore specialises in international books on nature and culture and everything below the mainstream radar, like books on counterculture or drugs, but also very high-quality children's books. They serve damn good coffee as well. A real gem in a lovely, lively neighbourhood.

236 OCELOT

239 BÜCHERBOGEN AM SAVIGNYPLATZ

238 ANOTHER COUNTRY

Riemannstrasse 7
Kreuzberg ②
+49 (0)30 6940 1160
anothercountry.de

A very unique English bookstore you'll probably remember forever. Some of the books are for sale, some for rent. Shopkeeper Sophia has probably read them all. She also hosts readings and writing workshops, often in cooperation with The Reader Berlin. In the basement you'll find a wide selection of science fiction and fantasy novels.

239 BÜCHERBOGEN AM SAVIGNYPLATZ

Stadtbahnbogen 593
Charlottenburg ⑨
+49 (0)30 3186 9511
buecherbogen-shop.de

This big art bookstore (with a huge English section) is located straight under the overground railway in the middle of the pleasant Savignyplatz. The focus is on art, design, fashion and photography and there's a unique collection of art exhibition catalogues from 1945 on. The store won the Deutscher Buchhandlungspreis (German Bookstore Price) in 2015. They also host film evenings, readings and expositions.

240 CURIOUS FOX

Lausitzer Platz 17
Kreuzberg ②
curiousfoxbooks.com

You can find new and used books in this English bookshop that recently moved from Neukölln to Kreuzberg. An independent and unique bookstore that has a really good eye for local talent as well. They also organise readings and other super nice activities for reading addicts: check their website!

5 shops for
UNUSUAL GIFTS

---

241 INTERNATIONAL WARDROBE

Almstadtstrasse 50
Mitte ①
+49 (0)30 5017 7671
*international
wardrobe.com*

International Wardrobe was founded in 2009 by the art historian, ethnologist and stylist Katharina Koppenwallner. She collects and buys traditional clothing and objects from around the world and sells these unique pieces to an international and trendy clientele. Most of it is handmade and absolutely gorgeous!

242 DEUTSCHE SPIRITUOSEN MANUFAKTUR

Brunnenstrasse 163
Mitte ③
+49 (0)30 9858 7232
d-s-m.com

This is the showroom and shop of DSM. Each one of their spirits is made in Berlin; handcrafted and 100% pure. I especially love the apothecary bottles they use for their unique herb and vegetable spirits. Every first Friday of the month, a guided tour of the distillery (situated in Marzahn) starts at 2 pm. Highly recommended!

243 S.WERT

Brunnenstrasse 191
Mitte ①
+49 (0)176 2956 7794
s-wert-design.de

You can feel the love for Berlin in every object on display in this shop that looks like a mix of an art gallery and a designer boutique. From the cushions to the postcards, everything you see here is designed in Berlin. Definitely go if you love Berlin's brutalist architecture.

244 BELYZIUM

Lottumstrasse 15
Mitte ①
+49 (0)30 4404 6484
belyzium.com

At Belyzium Berlin they take chocolate very seriously, following up everything from A to Z – from growing and processing the (organic) cacaobeans in Southern Belize, over shipping them to Germany to making chocolate right in the centre of Berlin. Their products are all organic and vegan.

245 SOUQ BERLIN

Kollwitzstrasse 54
Prenzlauer Berg ③
+49 173 6494 994
souqdukkan.de

Souq was founded as a vintage bazaar in 2014 in Turkey and quickly became a hub for young designers, artists and craftspeople that finally had a place where they could sell their art. We are very lucky to have them now in Berlin as well. Here you can find carefully hand-picked products from all over the world. From ceramics over homeware or plants or accessories... everything is beautiful!

244 BELYZIUM

The 5 best
CONTEMPORARY
DESIGN *shops*

---

246 GEYERSBACH

Kopenhagener Str. 17
Prenzlauer Berg ③
+49 (0)176 6416 7571
geyersbach.com

This furniture shop takes upcycling and recycling to another level. Old doors are turned into lockers, old floors into tables. It's all very beautiful, ecological, one-of-a-kind and soulful. Ulf and Katia Geyersbach have a passion for old pinewood that they mainly salvage from old abandoned buildings.

247 S7-STORE

Max-Beer-Strasse 25
Mitte ①
+49 (0)30 3087 2074
siebensachen.com

Siebensachen is the baby of Adam+Harborth. Both these product designers design games, musical boxes and other items under their own names, but they also work for various international brands. Their designs are timeless with a twist, and made out of carefully selected materials.

248 HALLESCHES HAUS

Tempelhofer Ufer 1
Kreuzberg ②
+49 (0)176 8413 8777
hallescheshaus.com

Everything in this former post office is selected with the greatest care and style. Most of the products are refined versions of everyday objects. And the owners added a range of high-quality and beautifully-packed groceries that are also used in the cafe. They serve an excellent lunch that changes every day.

250 AMODO

248 HALLESCHES HAUS

249 THE DISTRICT SIX STORE

Graefestrasse 80
Kreuzberg ②
+49 (0)30 2845 6216
districtsix.de

Caroline Adam is a graphic designer from Berlin who decided to open this small and cosy concept store to combine her love for South Africa with her love for interior design. She sells mostly fairtrade South African design – from interior accessories and carefully selected South African art pieces, to jewellery and even wallpaper.

250 AMODO

Linienstrasse 150
Mitte ①
+49 (0)30 3116 9474
amodoberlin.com

Once you're inside this shop, you enter another world. There's a beautiful selection of Italian and international designer items like Icelandic beauty products or delicate handcrafted ceramics. Italian owner Marianne runs her shop with a passion too many shopkeepers lack nowadays.

The 5 best shops for
VINTAGE CLOTHING

251 MIMI

Goltzstrasse 5
Schöneberg ⑦
+49 (0)30 2363 8438
mimi.berlin

Probably the best vintage shop in town. Behind the mini shop window you'll find 160 m² of fabulous vintage clothing. Rico and Mirjam Gresen also rent out clothes, accessories and suitcases made between 1800 and 1950, with an emphasis on the twenties and thirties. Think of Kate Winslet's outfits in *The Reader* or the costumes in *Inglorious Bastards* and you know what quality to expect.

252 LET THEM EAT CAKE

Weserstrasse 164
Neukölln ⑥
+49 (0)30 6096 5095

The name of this vintage and project space in trendy Neukölln comes from a line supposedly uttered by Marie Antoinette. The shop features a top-notch selection of vintage and second-hand clothes. It's not super cheap, but the nice clothes and the graceful look of the space make a visit worthwhile.

253 HUMANA

Frankfurter Tor 3
Friedrichshain ④
+49 (0)30 4222 018
humana-
second-hand.de

The Humana stores are part of a humanitarian organisation with twelve outlets at different locations in the city. You can find the biggest one near the Frankfurter Tor U-bahn (U5) in Friedrichshain. Here you'll find 2000 m² of second-hand, cheap clothes spread over four floors. It's vintage heaven – or hell, depending on your perception.

254 CACHE CŒUR

Schönhauser Allee 174
Prenzlauer Berg ③
+49 (0)30 4435 4962
cachecoeur.de

This store always looks like a work in progress but Gerlinde, the shopkeeper, makes up for that because she runs the shop with passion. The high-class clothes (mostly from the second half of the 20th century and often haute couture) are almost all in a flawless condition.

255 GLENCHECK

Joachim-Friedrich-
Strasse 34
Wilmersdorf
+49 (0)30 8912 199
glencheck-berlin.de

One doesn't think of independent and unique boutiques or of vintage shops when thinking of former West Berlin. However, there is this small hidden gem, run by Constanze Pelzer, who is dressed to forties perfection. It has been around for more than twenty years already. She sells a fantastic collection of rare vintage finds from the 1920s to 1950s.

The 5 most inspiring
JEWELLERY SHOPS

256 RENÉ TALMON L'ARMÉE

Linienstrasse 109
Mitte ①
+49 (0)30 9559 8446
renetalmonlarmee.com

René Talmon worked in Paris for Hermès and other houses before opening his first shop in the French capital. In 2011 Berlin followed. Talmon's jewellery features a lot of grey and black diamonds, and he also likes to work with oxidised silver and 18-carat or 22-carat gold. The pieces are cutting-edge and unique and very steampunk-like.

257 OONA GALERIE

Auguststrasse 26
Mitte ①
+49 (0)30 2804 45905
oona-galerie.de

Another very nice and unconventional shop in the trendy Mitte district is Oona. This is a gallery for contemporary jewellery really, of which the value can't be defined in terms of gold or stones. Instead, it's all about the artistic expression they carry. The space itself is stunning and bright and the works are beautifully exposed.

258 MICHAELA BINDER

Gipsstrasse 13
Mitte ⓘ
+49 (0)30 2838 4869
michaelabinder.de

Michaela Binder is a friendly, helpful and extremely passionate goldsmith. In her shop and atelier in Berlin Mitte she invites you to wander through her colourful world. Her bestseller is a ring or necklace made of different colourful pieces that you can buy separately and then combine.

259 QUITE QUIET

Auguststrasse 74
Mitte ⓘ
+49 (0)30 2392 7102
quite-quiet.com

Another awesome boutique in the cosy Auguststrasse. Quite Quiet was established in late 2016 by goldsmith Johanna Schoemaker and Jonas Buck, who believe that craftsmanship, advanced technology, esthetics and sustainability go hand in hand. The jewellery itself is sophisticated; we absolutely love the fine woven gold wire collection.

260 TUKADU

Rosenthalerstr. 46
Mitte ⓘ
+49 (0)30 2836 770
tukadu.com

Tukadu is unlike every other jewellery shop you've ever seen. Think of a huge selection of beads, plastic animals, mini clothes, small metal tags, ribbons and pompoms, all sorted by colour. Compose your own crazy piece or just grab one of the ready mades. The place is often crowded with tourists that are visiting the Haeckescher Courtyards and the whole district, so try to stop by before noon.

5 *exclusive*
FASHION SHOPS FOR WOMEN

261 TO.MTO

Torstrasse 22
Mitte ①
+49 (0)30 9700 4733
tomto.de

TO.mTO is Tonia Merz, a designer who is passionate about corsets, particularly the kind where fetishism and fashion meet. Every single piece is manufactured by hand in the Berlin workshop, which of course comes with a price. Most of Berlin's burlesque dancers are (very satisfied) customers.

262 REDCAT 7

Revaler Strasse 16/I
Friedrichshain ④
+49 (0)173 2468 920
redcat7.de

Redcat 7 is the brainchild of Berlin designer Sammy the Scissors. Think burlesque fashion, the crazy Weimar era and hot pin-up girls from the fifties and you get an idea of what Redcat 7 is about. You can also ask for something totally custom-made. So very Berlin!

263 APARTMENT BERLIN

Memhardstrasse 8
Mitte ①
+49 (0)30 2804 2251
apartmentberlin.de

Take the stairs and enter the dark world of minimal, urban fashion. Rick Owens, Cheap Monday, Vladimir Karaleev and Augustin Teboul are just a few of the designers and brands that are present here. They also have a nice selection of accessories.

264 DSTM

Torstrasse 161
Mitte ①
+49 (0)30 4920 3750
dstm.co

DSTM is the label of Canadian designer Jen Gilpin with a very unique and recognisable style: all black, articulated and sculptural. Gilpin loves the contrast of soft and hard shapes and she works only with ecological materials of the highest quality. Her clothes are unique and sometimes balance on the fine line between bodywear and ready-to-wear; they're sexy, slightly provocative and elegant.

265 ISABEL VOLLRATH

Linienstrasse 149
Mitte ①
+49 (0)30 5034 7280
isabelvollrath.com

Isabel Vollrath is a young fashion-and costume designer. She has worked (amongst many others) for the Max Gorki theatre and the Sasha Waltz Dance company. I'VR is the name of her own collection. Her clothes are far from ordinary and often dramatic and poetic. Just go and meet her in her atelier/shop. It's open from Monday to Saturday from 1 pm to 6 pm and by appointment.

The 5 best
FASHION SHOPS
FOR MEN

---

266 EGON BRANDSTETTER

Chausseestrasse 50
Mitte ①
+49 (0)30 9561 8383
egonbrandstetter.de

Brandstetter is a tailor, and a very good one indeed. One who really listens when his customers explain what they want. He makes bespoke suits for men, and everything is done by hand. With that kind of service comes a certain price, but you'll have a suit that will last a lifetime.

267 TRÜFFELSCHWEIN BERLIN

Rosa-Luxemburg-
Strasse 21
Mitte ①
+49 (0)30 7022 1225
*trueffelschwein
berlin.com*

Trüffelschwein (the name means 'truffle pig') is a nice alternative for the often hype-driven menswear stores in Berlin. They have a nice collection of small niche as well as more established brands like Hansen or Superga. The shop itself has a very unique aesthetic to it and the service here is excellent and personal.

268 DARKLANDS

Lindower Strasse 22
Wedding ⑩
darklandsberlin.com

This shop is as hidden as it gets. You have to check their website to find the address and to book an appointment. The location, which changes periodically, is always unconventional. It's perfect for men who can appreciate real craftsmanship and excellent materials.

269 STEREOKI

Gabriel-Max-Strasse 18
Friedrichshain ④
+49 (0)30 5379 4667
stereoki.com

At Stereoki you'll find an appealing mix of big-name brands and small-label clothing. They stock lesser-known brands here like Libertine or Six Pack France and more obvious labels like New Balance and (the ecological label) Nudie jeans, and they have a full head-to-toe product assortment.

270 FEIN UND RIPP

Kastanienallee 91
Prenzlauer Berg ③
+49 (0)30 4403 3250
feinundripp.de

One day, a father and his two sons found a pile of button shirts, undershirts, and other men's clothing dating from the 1920s to the 1980s, in a factory near Stuttgart. They decided to open a store to bring all this to the public. Today this company stands out because of its love for durability. They only stock a few brands like Schiesser (underwear) or Trabert (working boots) that meet their high standards.

268 DARKLANDS

The 5 best
SNEAKER and
SHOE SHOPS

---

271 STICKABUSH // STAB BERLIN

Friedelstrasse 52
Neukölln ⑥
+49 (0)30 2021 5445
stickabush.com

This rather small shop always has its finger on the pulse when it comes to finding the latest and most wanted sneakers. The shop also offers a selection of caps, beanies and other cool accessories of brands like Carhartt, Ransom, Converse, New Balance, Herschel or Stussy.

272 AEYDE

Strausberger Platz 19
Friedrichshain ④
+49 (0)30 9153 3499
aeyde.com

The timeless shoes you'll find here are all handmade in Italy. Prices are very good value – you'll pay less than 200 euros for a high-heeled open-toe slingback sandal in nappa-leather for example, because Aeyde buys directly from the manufacturer.

273 OVERKILL

Köpenicker
Strasse 195-A
Kreuzberg ②
+49 (0)30 6107 6633
overkillshop.com

If street style is your thing, then this shop in trendy Kreuzberg is the place to be. Overkill has an excellent selection of international sneaker brands for men, women and kids, with lots of limited and retro editions and even vegan options. They also offer a nice selection of apparel and gadgets.

274 SOLEBOX

Nürnberger Str. 14
Charlottenburg ⑨
+49 (0)30 9120 6690
solebox.com

This rather small shop is supposed to be one of the best sneaker places in the world, thanks to their collaboration with famous sneaker brands. Some shoes, the Converse Modern Collection for example, are exclusively for sale in their store in Berlin.

275 ZEHA BERLIN

Prenzlauer Allee 213
Prenzlauer Berg ③
+49 (0)30 4401 7214
zeha-berlin.de

In the 1960s everyone in the GDR wore Zeha sneakers. The brand didn't survive the economical chaos after the Wall came down but when it was relaunched in 2002 it was an immediate success: everyone seems to love their retro look. They also have shops in Kreuzberg and Schöneberg.

5 hot

SEX SHOPS

276 SCHWARZER REITER

Torstrasse 3
Mitte ①
+49 (0)30 4503 4438
schwarzer-reiter.com

Not the cheapest sex shop but probably the most beautiful one. Inside there's a nice collection of luxury erotic stuff, from latex dresses to glass dildos. The shop owner, Sabine Schwarz, is also the designer of the Schwarzer Reiter Black label – a line of erotic clothes and accessories.

277 GORGEOUS

Schönhauser
Allee 130
Prenzlauer Berg ③
+49 (0)30 2520 4848
gorgeous-berlin.de

Gorgeous is a funny, sweet and low-threshold sex shop. If you want to bring some kinky souvenirs from Berlin, this toyshop for adults is the place to be. Open from 11 am to 8 pm.

278 OTHER NATURE

Mehringdamm 79
Kreuzberg ②
+49 (0)30 2091 5887
other-nature.de

Very Berlin-like: this is a so-called alternative sex shop. It is queer-friendly, vegan (no leather, no glycerine), eco-friendly (no parabens) and definitely feminist. They have an interesting selection of books about sexuality and lust.

279 MISTER B

Motzstrasse 22
Schöneberg ⑦
+49 (0)30 2199 7704
misterb.com

Mister B opened his first gay fetish shop in 1994 in Amsterdam. Their stock of leather goods is very extensive, and they offer the service of custom made-to-measure leather clothing for clients with special requirements. The staff is really friendly and helpful.

280 HAUTNAH BERLIN

Uhlandstrasse 170
Charlottenburg ⑨
+49 (0)30 8823 434
hautnahberlin.de

Three floors of extravagant fetish and erotic wear in lacquer, latex and leather: that's Hautnah. The choice is huge. A unique highlight is their wine cellar Marquis de Sade. If you're planning a night out in the KitKatClub or the Insomnia, then this is where you can find an outfit.

278 OTHER NATURE

The 5 most
SECRET SHOPPING DISTRICTS

---

281 AROUND THE MULACKSTRASSE

Mitte ①

This sidestreet of the Alte Schönhauser Strasse is one of the best streets to shop if you're into avant-garde design and if you like independent boutiques. Make sure to stop by Butterflysoulfire and fall in love with their own collection and their wonderful selection of design objects by international and local designers and artists. Tired of (window) shopping? Grab lunch at The Klub Kitchen (number 15).

282 AROUND THE WÜHLISCHSTRASSE

Friedrichshain ④

Friedrichshain is a young and funky district that might look a little less posh and leafy than districts like Prenzlauer Berg or Mitte, but it has some really cool, small independent shops – you just need to know where to look. The whole area is very pleasant to stroll through and you might find the perfect present at Stadtengel (number 24). The former sports hall Die Turnhalle (Wühlischplatz) is the place to be for an awesome brunch or a perfectly mixed cocktail.

283 AREA AROUND THE GOLTZSTRASSE

Schöneberg ⑦

On this sidestreet of the Winterfeldplatz you'll find cool and stylish shops like Down by Retro and super trendy bars. If you're hungry we recommend Gottlob (on the corner of the Akazienstrasse) and if you're in the mood for coffee have it served in a fifties cup, in the retro bar and former butchery Sorgenfrei (number 18).

284 SUAREZSTRASSE

Charlottenburg ⑨

With over thirty antique stores this is heaven for people who are into antiquities, vintage furniture and vintage clothing. A streetfest called Antikmeile (Antiques Mile) takes place here every first Saturday of September and attracts more than 30.000 visitors each year. For excellent German cuisine, find a table at the Engelbecken restaurant on the corner of the Kantstrasse.

285 DUNCKERSTRASSE

Prenzlauer Berg ③

The leafy streets of Prenzlauer Berg are lined with hundreds of nice bars, restaurants and shops as well as parks and hidden places (the Jewish cemetery for example, on the Schönhauser Allee). The area around the Dunckerstrasse is particularly charming. Here you'll find one of the best bakeries in town called Bekarei (number 23).

281 MULACKSTRASSE

284 SUAREZSTRASSE

5

ONE OF A KIND

shops

---

286 BLUMENCAFE

Schönhauser
Allee 127-A
Prenzlauer Berg ③
+49 (0)30 4473 4226
blumencafe-berlin.de

This place looks like the winter garden of your old, almost forgotten and eccentric aunt. A parallel green world in the city, that's another way to describe it. It is also a flower shop and a bar where the breakfast is pretty good. And it's also the house of Erwin the third, the housecat, and parrots Arno and Charly. Open 365 days a year.

287 BÜRSTEN-SCHRÖDER

Heimstrasse 22
Kreuzberg ③
+49 (0)173 6056 202
*buersten
schroeder1866.de*

Bürsten-Schröder is a manufacturer of brooms and brushes. The brushmaker who used to have his showroom here in the nineteenth century was famous for the creation of his anal brush. If you're looking for more regular brushes and/or a place where they sell this stuff, try DIM 26 on the Oranienstrasse 26.

288 KUBORAUM

Köpenicker Strasse 96
Mitte ①
+49 (0)30 2236 75499
kuboraum.com

This impressive flagship store is housed in a former post office. Kuboraum is a sunglasses brand, but here they call them "masks that are drawn on the face of the wearer, masks that highlight your personality, that highlight your character". Every pair of glasses is designed in Berlin, sometimes in collaboration with Japanese designers, and handmade in Italy.

289 ANTIQUE JEWELLERY

Linienstrasse 44
Mitte ①
+49 (0)30 2068 9155
antique-jewellery.de

Art historian Oliver Rheinfrank opened this shop about 20 years ago. Since then it has grown into one of the largest selections of antique jewellery in Europe. In the showroom you'll find more than 3000 original pieces dating mainly from 1750 until 1970. While shopping for your very special Victorian wedding ring you might be lucky and spot a Hollywood star.

290 ABSINTH DEPOT

Weinmeisterstrasse 4
Mitte ①
+49 (0)30 2816 789
absinthdepot.de

In the Absinth Depot you can find more than 100 varieties of absinth, the strong alcoholic drink that's also known as 'the Green Fairy'. The walls here are covered with patterned, gold lame wallpaper and period propaganda telling you "you will be alright". Michael Schöll, the shop owner, is always happy to introduce you to various kinds of absinth, and to present their history and quality features.

VIEW FROM A BRIDGE

60 PLACES TO DISCOVER THE BERLIN SPIRIT

The 5 most beautiful
BRIDGES

---

291 OBERBAUM BRIDGE
Friedrichshain-
Kreuzberg ②

There are more bridges in Berlin than in Venice – more than 950 that is. One of the most beautiful ones is the Oberbaum-brücke (built in 1895 with North-German Gothic brick) that connects the old East and the old West. When the Wall came down in 1989, the 154-metre-long bridge was restored to its former glory, but with a new middle section in steel.

292 GLIENICKE BRIDGE
Steglitz-Zehlendorf
& Potsdam

This small bridge across the Havel river connects the Wannsee district of Berlin with the Brandenburg capital Potsdam. The bridge is also known as the bridge where spies were exchanged during the Cold War. It's in fact the 'Bridge of Spies' that takes centre stage in the Steven Spielberg film with that title.

294 ADMIRAL BRIDGE

293 MONBIJOU BRIDGE

291 OBERBAUM BRIDGE

293 BRIDGES AROUND THE MUSEUM ISLAND
Mitte ①

The five museums on the Museum Island in the city centre, a sanctuary of art and science, were built between 1824 and 1930 and they're on the Unesco World Heritage List. They are accessible by different bridges; the Palace Bridge (Schlossbrücke), designed by Schinkel, and the Monbijou Bridge in the north are the most beautiful ones.

294 ADMIRAL BRIDGE
Kreuzberg ②

This is a very small bridge across the Landwehrkanal. It has a Parisian feel to it and on a warm summer evening it's the definition of romance in a big city, for many Berliners as well as tourists. Spontaneous parties can occur, and it's also famous for its buskers.

295 MODERSOHN BRIDGE
Friedrichshain ③

This bridge has a completely different vibe than the ones mentioned above: this one is all about rusty steal and a skyline with (too) many cranes, reminding you that Berlin is still a city under construction. Many young people come here at sundown to sip a beer and enjoy the urban landscape.

5 typical
BERLIN PARKS

296 VIKTORIAPARK
Kreuzbergstrasse
Kreuzberg ②

Viktoriapark is a historic wine-growing area and also proud to be the park with the highest hill in Berlin: 66 metres! Don't hesitate to climb up there; you will find a national monument for the Napoleonic wars designed by Schinkel that provides a really nice view over the city. In summer an artificial waterfall rises at the foot of the monument.

297 GÄRTEN DER WELT
Eisenacher Strasse 99
Marzahn
+49 (0)30 7009 06699
gruen-berlin.de/
gaerten-der-welt

These grounds were cultivated as a gift from the gardeners to the capital of the GDR in 1987. Now it's an amazing park with a Chinese, Japanese and Italian garden as well as a paved labyrinth. You can even take part in a traditional Chinese tea ceremony and get an introduction to the philosophical, spiritual and aesthetic qualities of a cup of chá.

297 **GÄRTEN DER WELT**

298 NATUR-PARK SÜDGELÄNDE

Prellerweg 47-49
Schöneberg ⑦
+49 (0)30 7009 0624
gruen-berlin.de/natur-
park-suedgelaende

This used to be an old railway yard, but fifty years ago it was converted into a small park. It's very young but very interesting, partly because of the mix of wild nature and old industrial architecture, like the water tower or the former locomotive hall (which is popular with artists). There's a bar that opens every weekend in summer.

299 WEISSENSEE JEWISH CEMETERY

Herbert-Baum-Str. 45
Weissensee
+49 (0)30 9253 330
jewish-cemetery-
weissensee.org

There are many Jewish cemeteries in Berlin but this one is really special. It's no less than 42 hectares big and has more than 115.000 graves, which makes it the largest Jewish cemetery in Europe and a cultural and historic landmark. Its completely preserved death registry is a unique historical document that tells the story of the development of Berlin's Jewish community.

300 CHARLOTTENBURG PALACE GARDENS

Spandauer Damm
Charlottenburg ⑨
+49 (0)33 1969 4200
spsg.de/en/palaces-
gardens/object/
charlottenburg-palace-
gardens

The garden park was laid out in 1697 as the first baroque garden in Germany. A stroll around the 55 hectares that showcase beautiful historical garden architecture can easily be combined with a visit to the palace. Across the street of the palace there are two museums, the Bröhan Museum, specialised in art nouveau and art deco, and the exquisite Berggruen Museum, which houses modern art.

The 5 best
FLEA MARKETS

---

301 ANTIQUES AND BOOK MARKET NEAR THE BODE-MUSEUM

Am Kupfergraben 1
Mitte ①
+49 (0)171 7101 662
antik-buchmarkt.de

Be it winter or summer, it's always a pleasure to stroll around Kupfergraben and shop for bargains at the different stalls. Start at the Bode-Museum and move up to Unter den Linden. In front of the Humboldt University, books are getting more international and scientific. Saturdays and Sundays, 10 am till 5 pm.

302 MAUERPARK

Prenzlauer Berg ③
flohmarktim
mauerpark.de

Chances are low you will find a bargain, but it's surely the youngest, most hipster and most international flea market in Berlin. The famous karaoke, food stalls and buskers are absolutely worth the trip.

303 ARKONAPLATZ

Prenzlauer Berg ③
+49 (0)171 7101 662
troedelmarkt-
arkonaplatz.de

A large selection of books, old sound systems, Bakelite telephones and diverse vintage furniture will be lying there under the trees waiting for buyers. It takes place every Sunday from 10 am to 6 pm. For a lovely breakfast, go to café Der Neue Weltempfaenger.

304 LEOPOLDPLATZ FLEA MARKET

SATURDAYS: 9 AM – 3 PM

Wedding ⑩

This is a less well-known flea market in Berlin that takes place in front of the Alter Nazareth Church on the Leopoldplatz. It's multicultural and authentic, and celebrated for the vast and kaleidoscopic range of paraphernalia it has on offer. Tassenkuchen or Schraders are recommended if you want to have brunch nearby.

305 NOWKOELLN FLOWMARKT

Maybachufer 31

Neukölln ⑥

nowkoelln.de

This huge but cosy flea market takes place every second Sunday of the month (not in winter, though). Just head over to idyllic Maybachufer, a leafy promenade in the centre of Kreuzkölln. This market specialises in used goods, art and original handicrafts. A very *Berlinish*, uncomplicated atmosphere and good buskers too!

305 NOWKOELLN FLOWMARKT

5 MOVIES

from after 1989 that were shot entirely in Berlin

---

306 RUN LOLA RUN (LOLA RENNT)
TOM TYKWER, 1998
With Franka Potente and Moritz Bleibtreu.

An action thriller in which the red-haired Lola (Franka Potente) runs against time through the city of Berlin to come up with 100.000 marks to save her boyfriend Manni (Moritz Bleibtreu) after he botched a money delivery. Three different alternatives may happen depending on some minor event along Lola's run. Includes a fabulous shot on the Oberbaum Bridge.

307 GOOD BYE, LENIN!
WOLFGANG BECKER, 2003
With Daniel Brühl and Katrin Sass

This feel-good film shows the beginning of the end of communism in Berlin and the destruction of the Wall through the eyes of young Alex. To protect his fragile mother from a fatal shock after a long coma, he must keep her from learning that her beloved nation, East Germany as she knew it, has disappeared.

308 THE LIVES OF OTHERS (DAS LEBEN DER ANDEREN)
FLORIAN HENCKEL VON DONNERSMARCK, 2006
With Ulrich Mühe and Martina Gedeck

The story told in this political thriller begins in East Berlin in 1984, five years before the end of communism in Europe, and ends in 1991. The film traces the gradual disillusionment of Gerd Wiesle, a member of the Stasi, East Germany's all-powerful secret police, whose mission is to spy on a celebrated writer and actress couple.

309 A COFFEE IN BERLIN (OH BOY)
JAN-OLE GERSTER, 2012
With Tom Schilling and Friederike Kempter

A tragicomedy and self-ironic portrait of a young man who drops out of university and ends up wandering the streets of Berlin. He tries to participate in life but struggles to find his place. The tension between the black comedy and the underlying backdrop of Berlin's inescapable history is knife-edged. Filmed in black and white, the film has a certain Nouvelle Vague feel.

310 VICTORIA
SEBASTIAN SCHIPPER, 2015
With Laia Costa and Frederick Lau

This film follows exchange student Victoria (Laia Costa) on a dark night out with a band of criminal Berliners. It was shot in Berlin in one continuous, uninterrupted take with a small cast and crew, in the wee small hours (from around 4.30 am to 7 am) on April 27, 2014. Fantastic score by Nils Frahm.

5 places with a strong
G D R   V I B E

---

311 CENTRAL CEMETERY FRIEDRICHSFELDE

(Memorial to the
Socialists)
Gudrunstrasse 20
Lichtenberg
+49 (0)30 9029 64224
sozialistenfriedhof.de

Karl Liebknecht and Rosa Luxemburg were buried at this magnificent graveyard in 1919. In 1951, the newly formed GDR government built the Socialist Memorial and began using the Zentralfriedhof as a place to hold state funerals. You'll also find pre-GDR luminaries such as artist Käthe Kollwitz. The grave of Stasi-leader Erich Mielke has been left unmarked intentionally.

312 STASI MUSEUM

Ruschestrasse 103
Lichtenberg
+49 (0)30 5536 854
stasimuseum.de

The Stasi Museum is located on the former grounds of the huge headquarters of the GDR Ministry for State Security. Centrepiece of the museum is the office of Stasi-chef Erich Mielke, preserved in its original condition. The permanent exposition 'State Security in the SED Dictatorship' provides information about the development, the function and the methods of the State Security.

313 PALACE OF TEARS / TRÄNENPALAST

Reichstagufer 17
Mitte ①
+49 (0)30 4677 7790
hdg.de/berlin/
traenenpalast

This was the main departure point for travellers (who shed more than one tear) from the former East Germany to West Berlin. The museum explains the role of this frontier post, as well as the complicated politics and the history behind it. Free entrance.

314 BERLIN TV-TOWER / FERNSEHTURM

Alexanderplatz
Panoramastrasse 1-A
Mitte ①
tv-turm.de

The 368-metre-high TV-tower was constructed in the late sixties by the GDR administration. It was intended as a symbol of the technological superiority of the socialist societies. Now it's a symbol of unity and Berlin's most prominent landmark. You can visit its steel sphere, which holds a visitor platform and a restaurant.

315 KARL-MARX-ALLEE

Mitte /
Friedrichshain ①

This street used to be called 'Stalin Allee' and dates from the post-war reconstruction of the Soviet occupied zones of Berlin. It was built to represent the socialist ideals of the New Germany. Most of the buildings in socialist-realist (or 'wedding cake') style are protected as landmarks. Don't miss the Karl Marx Bookshop at number 78.

5 astonishing
STREET-ART SPOTS

316 RAW GELÄNDE
Along Revalerstrasse
Friedrichshain ④

This old train repair centre is now one of the last subcultural compounds in central Berlin. This graffiti-filled space also harbours clubs, bars, a swimming pool club, an indoor skate park, a flea market and a bunker-turned-climbing-wall.

317 KREUZBERG
Entire neighbourhood
Kreuzberg ②

Kreuzberg was always at the centre of Berlin's alternative scene, which explains why there is a lot of politically motivated street art here. The highlights of this area are the firewalls with huge murals on them. *Take the Spaceman*, for example: it's one of the largest stencils in the world, tagged by the French artist Victor Ash.

318 HAUS SCHWARZENBERG
Rosenthalerstr. 39
Mitte ①
+49 (0)30 3087 2573
haus-schwarzenberg.org

The whole of Haus Schwarzenberg and its courtyard manages to maintain its postwar state. It houses shops, a club, an independent cinema and two museums. What triggers the interest of street art enthusiasts are the stunning works of famous street artists like D Screet, Jimmy C or El Bocho.

319 TAGESZEITUNG (TAZ)

"Friede sei mit Dir"
(May peace be
with you)
Rudi-Dutschke-
Strasse 23
Kreuzberg ②

Kai Diekmann, the right-wing editor of *Bild Zeitung*, sued the leftist TAZ for libel after it 'reported' in its satire column that Diekmann had a penis enlargement surgery, "but the operation went badly and resulted in castration". Diekmann lost and TAZ installed a sculpture of Diekmann, with a six-metre-long penis, on the side of their building, which is across the street from Bild's building.

320 URBAN NATION

Museum for Urban
Contemporary Art
Bülowstrasse 7
Schöneberg ⑦
urban-nation.com

The area around Bülowstrasse used to be grey and a bit dodgy – until September 2017, when this museum came to life. The whole area now looks like an open-air museum, thanks to the many painted façades. Truly amazing! Entrance to the museum is free but booking a guided tour is strongly encouraged.

320 URBAN NATION

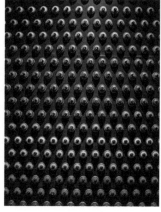

The 5 most
ICONIC STATUES

---

321 SOVIET MEMORIAL TREPTOW

Treptower Park
Puschkinallee
Alt-Treptow ⑤

Traces of the recent past are everywhere in Berlin. This is one of the three military memorials for the millions of Soviet soldiers that were killed in World War II. It's located in the beautiful Treptower Park and with its 100.000 m² it's pretty impressive.

322 GERMAN RESISTANCE MEMORIAL CENTER

Stauffenbergstr. 13-14
Tiergarten ⑧
+49 (0)30 2699 5000
gdw-berlin.de

This museum is located in the house where Hitler delivered his speech on *Lebensraum* (living space). The commemorative courtyard is dedicated to the memory of the officers that attempted to overthrow the National Socialist regime and were executed here on the night of July 20, 1944.

323 MEMORIAL TO THE SINTI AND ROMA VICTIMS

Simsonsweg
Tiergarten ⑧
+49 (0)30 2639 430

Tiergarten, the former hunting grounds of the kings, is the biggest park in Berlin. It houses the impressive and sober memorial dedicated to the memory of the 200.000 to 500.000 people who were murdered during the *Porajmos* – the Nazi genocide of the European Sinti and Roma.

321 SOVIET MEMORIAL TREPTOW

322 GERMAN RESISTANCE MEMORIAL CENTER

324 LARGE DIVIDED OVAL: BUTTERFLY BY HENRY MOORE

John-Foster-Dulles-
Allee 10
Mitte ①
+49 (0)30 3978 7175
hkw.de

Before visitors enter the Haus der Kulturen der Welt (The House of the World cultures, a venue for international contemporary arts) they stumble upon Henry Moore's last sculpture, erected in 1987: a giant butterfly, weighing over 8 tons, and yet it seems to hover weightlessly over the surface of the pool.

325 VIKTORIA/GOLDELSE

On top of the Victory
Column (Siegessäule)
Grosser Stern
Tiergarten ⑧

This 8,3-metre-high gilded female figure by Friedrich Drake weighs 35 ton and stands on top of the Victory Column in the middle of Tiergarten Park. It's also known as 'Goldelse' and represents the barefoot and winged Victoria, Goddess of Victory.

324 LARGE DIVIDED OVAL: BUTTERFLY BY HENRY MOORE

The 5 best
CO-WORKING SPACES

326 **BETAHAUS**
Rudi-Dutschke-
Strasse 23
Kreuzberg ②
+49 (0)30 2201 19820
betahaus.com

In a city where most people live in small apartments, co-working spaces are popular. Betahaus is Berlin's best known co-working space and probably the largest in Europe. It still manages to feel like a cool social club where hip night-time events take place on a regular basis.

327 **MINDSPACE**
Friedrichstrasse 68
Mitte ①
+49 (0)32 2111 22490
mindspace.me/c/berlin

This global flex workspace provider is conquering the world in no time. Their beautifully designed spaces couldn't be more different from some of the city's shabbier co-working offices. It comes with a (higher) price and is thus more suitable for companies or start-ups than for the many self-employed people in Berlin.

328 **AGORA**
Am Sudhaus 2
Neukölln ⑥
+49 (0)30 9954 8264
agoracollective.org

Agora Collective's art space is in a former brewery in hipster Neukölln. The 1000-sqm location combines a co-working space and art studios. It's an ongoing experimental centre for sustainable and artistic practices. Once a month, there is an artist-run bar called Babes that is definitely worth checking out.

329 UNICORN

Brunnenstrasse 173
Mitte ①
+49 (0)30 2148 0660

This is co-working at its hippest. Unicorn provides high-end ecological co-working spaces and a fantastic cafe. Everything here is vegan, organic and if possible locally sourced, and it can be delivered to your home. Also nice is the small scale of this undertaking. Unicorn has two locations: one in Mitte and one in Wedding; they're in the same street (the Wedding location is at number 64).

330 AHOY! BERLIN

Wattstrasse 11
Charlottenburg ⑨
+49 (0)30 2084 9740
ahoyberlin.com

Ahoy! is a huge, airy and light 4500 m² space that has brought some much-needed cool to the West. An extra bonus is the floor where you can have some fun during your break, including billiards, a punch bag and table tennis.

329 UNICORN

The 5 best
GUIDED TOURS

---

331 DOGGY BAG TOURS

Pohlstrasse 43
Tiergarten ⑧
+49 (0)176 4767 8220
doggybagtours.com

Why not explore Berlin by bike? Doggy Bag Tours is one of the smallest tour operators but the Dutch founders know literally everything about their adopted city. On the Hidden Berlin tour for instance, you will visit the places where East meets West, explore Kreuzberg with its protesters and street art, and ride your bike on the runway of a former airport that used to be a Third Reich landmark.

332 GREEN FASHION TOURS

+49 (0)163 6852 985
greenfashiontours.com

If you're interested in sustainable fashion, this is the guide you should turn to. The tours will take you to the most interesting sustainable fashion and upcycling spots in town. You will also get the exclusive chance to get to know designers and concept store founders personally. Different themes are offered, as well as styling consultancy.

333 BERLIN UNDERWORLDS

Brunnenstrasse 105
Mitte ③
+49 (0)30 4991 0517
berliner-unterwelten.de

The primary aim of Berliner Unterwelten is to explore and document the city's underground architecture and to make it accessible to the public. Underground means caverns, air raid shelters, disused railway tunnels, derelict brewery vaults and so on. They offer many different tours in many languages and they all are worth every cent. Older children will love this.

334 QUEER TOUR

Schöneberg ⑦
+49 (0)151 4011 2203
finn-ballard-tours.com

On this tour you will explore gay Schöneberg. You'll see Christopher Isherwood's home and visit the Eldorado, one of Europe's first gay and transgender meeting-spots. You will learn about the pioneer of 'Sexology' Hirschfeld, see the lesbian quarter of Weimar Berlin and so much more. Queer historian Finn Ballard is an expert on the subject. Not for children under 12.

335 STREET ART TOUR & WORKSHOP

MEETING POINT:
Alexanderplatz,
TV Tower
Mitte ①
+49 (0)162 8198 264
alternativeberlin.com

Alternative Berlin combines a tour on street art with a workshop on how to make your own urban art. You will learn about the history and the origins of this art form, the difference between street art and graffiti, the unwritten rules and codes of conduct etc. All the guides are street artists/ graffiti writers and experts on the subject. For kids older than 12.

The 5 places where you can still see some parts of the
BERLIN WALL

---

336 THE GDR WATCHTOWER

Erna-Berger-Strasse
Mitte ①
diemauerthewall.de

The Berlin Wall, built around West Berlin, was a reality people had to live with from 1961 to 1989. There were lots of guard towers too, and the guards had orders to shoot to kill everybody who wanted to escape. This tower is the last of the round 'mushroom'-type towers to remain standing and therefore a sad reminder of the past.

337 BERLIN WALL MEMORIAL

Bernauer Strasse 111
Mitte ③
+49 (0)30 4679 86666
berliner-mauer-gedenkstaette.de

If you want to understand how and why the Wall was built, this memorial and museum is an absolute must. It consists of the Visitor/ Documentation Centre and the Open-Air Exhibition and Memorial Grounds. There's also an exhibition called *Border Stations and Ghost Stations in Divided Berlin* in the Nordbahnhof S-Bahn station. Interesting guided tours.

337 BERLIN WALL MEMORIAL

338 TOPOGRAPHY OF TERROR

Niederkirchnerstr. 8
Kreuzberg ②
+49 (0)30 2545 0950
topographie.de

The Topography, which used to be the SS police station, is now a documentation centre about all the horrible acts that were committed in the Third Reich. The remaining 200 metres of the Wall at the Niederkirchnerstraße – which marked the border between East and West – have been preserved and now are part of the Topography of Terror Documentation Center. An absolute must!

339 THE WALL
ASISI PANORAMA BERLIN

Checkpoint Charlie
Friedrichstrasse 205
Kreuzberg ②
+49 (0)34 1355 5340
asisi.de

Checkpoint Charlie, the Berlin Wall crossing place that symbolises the Cold War, has degenerated into a seedy tourist trap. The 360° Asisi Panorama is a better option: you'll relive everyday life in the vicinity of the Berlin Wall on a fictitious autumn day in the 1980s. Don't miss the fine pictures of the fall of the Wall in the foyer.

340 LIESENSTRASSE

Mitte ①

Don't expect to find any tourists here. To be honest there's not much to see: no hipster shops, no museums, no bars, no memorials. But there is a piece of the Wall here, and it's intact and genuine – what they call a 'wild Wall'.

The 5 most
SECRET BACKYARDS

341 CAMARO FOUNDATION
Potsdamer Str. 98-A
Mitte ①
+49 (0)30 2639 2975
camaro-stiftung.de

Not only is Berlin a very green city where parks cover 30 percent of the city's surface, but it's also a city where one can find many courtyards. This private backyard houses the Camaro Foundation, so you might enjoy the beauty of a green backyard and attend an art exposition as well.

342 HECKMANN HÖFE
Oranienburger Str. 32
Mitte ①
+49 (0)30 3036 2580
heckmann-hoefe.de

This beautiful courtyard connects the Oranienburger Strasse with the Auguststrasse. In fact, the whole area is filled with hidden gems like this. There is of course the Hackesche Höfe, but also check the Sophie-Gips-Höfe (Sophienstrasse 21) and Kunstwerke (Auguststr. 69).

343 JEWISH MUSEUM
Glass courtyard
Lindenstrasse 9-14
Kreuzberg ②
+49 (0)30 2599 3300
jmberlin.de

Architect Daniel Libeskind added this enclosed courtyard, surrounded by glass, to the old building of the Jewish Museum in 2007. The starting point was a design entitled *Sukkah* (which is Hebrew for 'thatched booth'). In fact the roof of the new glass courtyard covers an area of 706 m².

344 MIETSKASERNEN IN WEDDING

Gerichtstrasse 23
Wedding ⑩

Mietskasernen (tenements) were built during times when the Berlin population grew sharply, mostly after the German unification in 1871. Those big tenements were required to have courtyards large enough for a fire truck to be able to turn around, and often the buildings enclose several courtyards. In the Gerichtstrasse many of those are in their original state, and they still have that unique Berlin urban atmosphere.

345 CAMERA WORK

Kantstrasse 149
Charlottenburg ⑨
+49 (0)30 3100 773
camerawork.de

Camera Work is a big photo gallery housed in a magnificent courtyard space. Combine a visit to the Gallery with a visit to the Museum for Photography (Helmut Newton Foundation) and the C/O Berlin in the America House (Hardenbergstrasse 22).

344 MIETSKASERNEN IN WEDDING

5 interesting
TATTOO ARTISTS
based in Berlin

---

346 **VALENTIN HIRSCH**
(ON APPOINTMENT ONLY)
Neukölln ⑥
valentinhirsch.com

Berlin is a tattoo-friendly city. It's impossible to say how many skilled tattooists this city counts, but one of the best is, without any doubt, Valentin Hirsch, who studied at the Academy of Fine Arts in Vienna. The unique animal designs of this obsessive draftsman are often symmetrical.

347 **ANDY MA**
AT: LIGHTWORKERS TATTOO
(ON APPOINTMENT ONLY)
Kreuzberg ②

Tattoo artist Andy MA founded this tattoo studio in Kreuzberg. He only uses vegan ink and 10 percent of the profit goes to animal rescue and animal rights groups. If you are a member of the Sea Shepherd ship crew then you will get your tattoos for free.

348 DOTSTOLINES
(ON APPOINTMENT ONLY)
dotstolines.com

Chaim Machlev is a one-of-a-kind artist. He started tattooing in 2012, completely inexperienced and with zero fine arts training. Nowadays he's one of the best-known tattoo artists in the world. Chaim claims a tattoo is an extension of the body. His fantastic blackwork is unique and can't be put in a box.

349 MARET BROTKRUMEN
(ON APPOINTMENT ONLY)
instagram.com/ lordenstein_art

Maret has an art degree and a passion for game art and anime, which is reflected in her often very detailed blackwork tattoos. Don't be fooled by the apparent naïveness of her designs: some of them are heartbreakingly beautiful.

350 EJSMONT & FENRIS
(ON APPOINTMENT ONLY)
Döringstrasse 7
Friedrichshain ④
axelejsmont.com

Axel Ejsmont is a Polish illustrator and tattoo artist. Her style could be described as minimalist and her tattoos look like she drew stuff in a sketchbook and then transferred it onto skin. Mirja Fenris has got a more graphic and art deco style. Both artists love symmetry, dots and complex designs.

BUCHSTABENMUSEUM

45 PLACES
TO ENJOY CULTURE

5 *interesting*
ART GALLERIES

———

351 **EIGEN + ART**
    Auguststrasse 26
    Mitte ①
    +49 (0)30 2806 605
    eigen-art.com

Galerie EIGEN + ART emerged in the year 1983 as an unofficial gallery project in the private loft of Gerd Harry Lybke in Leipzig (GDR). After the Wall came down, he opened a gallery in the (back then still seedy) Auguststrasse where he represented and represents mostly artists from the so-called 'New Leipzig School'.

352 **SAMMLUNG BOROS**
    (ON APPOINTMENT ONLY)
    Bunker
    Reinhardtstrasse 20
    Mitte ①
    +49 (0)30 2408 33300
    sammlung-boros.de

This is a bunker with a typical Berlin history: it was constructed by the Nazis, then turned into a camp for prisoners of war by the Russians, and then used as a warehouse (where bananas were stored) before being turned into a famous hardcore techno club. Now the building hosts the exquisite private selection of contemporary art of Christian Boros. Check the website and make a reservation for a guided visit or you won't get in!

353 MEINBLAU GALLERY

Christinenstr. 18-19
Prenzlauer Berg ③
+49 (0)30 4496 457
meinblau.de

MEINBLAU is an interesting and small project room. The space is often curated by the artists in residence or by other artist collectives, and has nothing to do with the commercial art market or the political mainstream. The gallery's position as a bulwark of independent art in this district is becoming more and more important as the neighbourhoods around it are becoming more and more gentrified.

354 POTSDAMER STRASSE

Tiergarten ⑧

The area around the Potsdamer Strasse seems to be becoming the new place to be for art lovers. The street has developed into a melting pot for contemporary art with already more than 30 galleries. If you're in need of a coffee, try Zimt und Zucker at number 103. Gorgeous!

355 HAUS AM WALDSEE

Argentinische
Allee 30
Zehlendorf
+49 (0)30 8018 935
hausamwaldsee.de

Although the House itself is much older, it was only launched as an exhibition space in 1946. Today it offers a platform for artists who live and work in Berlin and have already achieved significant international standing. There's a particular emphasis on reaching out to the public, which is why there are also events like yoga lessons amidst the art, artist's talks, etc. and there's a nice cafe as well.

The 5 best
ART MUSEUMS

356 **GEORG KOLBE MUSEUM**
Sensburger Allee 25
Charlottenburg ⑨
+49 (0)30 3042 144
georg-kolbe-museum.de

Kolbe was the most successful German sculptor of the first half of the twentieth century. Three years after his death in 1947, his studio became the first museum that opened in West Berlin. It is dedicated to the research and the preservation of Kolbe's artistic legacy and hosts interesting exhibitions. The place and its surroundings, including Café K, are simply magnificent.

357 **BERLINISCHE GALERIE**
Alte Jakobstrasse 124–128
Kreuzberg ②
+49 (0)30 7890 2600
berlinischegalerie.de

The 'Berlin Gallery' collects art from Berlin dating from 1870 to the present day, with both a local and international focus. It offers 4600 m² of exhibition space with outstanding collections that include Dada Berlin, the *Neue Sachlichkeit* (New Objectivity) and the Eastern European avant-garde. You can combine your visit with one to the Jewish Museum nearby.

358 MUSEUM FÜR FOTOGRAFIE

Jebensstrasse 2
Charlottenburg ⑨
+49 (0)30 2664 24242
smb.museum/en/
museums-institutions

The Museum of Photography,
a former officers' casino, is now home
to the Kunstbibliothek's Collection of
Photography and the Helmut Newton
Foundation. These two institutions have
2000 m² of exhibition space at their
disposal. As far as Helmut Newton's
multi-faceted and often provocative
work goes, it is presented in a series
of alternating exhibitions.

359 HAMBURGER BAHNHOF

Invalidenstrasse 50-51
Mitte ①
+49 (0)30 2664 24242
smb.museum/museen-
und-einrichtungen

The huge Hamburger Bahnhof is the
former railway station where trains left
and arrived on their way to or from the
Hanseatic city of Hamburg. It is now an
awesome museum for contemporary art.
Changing exhibits cover a wide range
of post-1950 artistic movements. The
permanent collection is world class;
think Joseph Beuys, Andy Warhol or
Cy Twombly.

360 KINDL - CENTRE FOR CONTEMPORARY ART

Am Sudhaus 3
Neukölln ⑥
+49 (0)30 8321 59120
kindl-berlin.com

KINDL is a beautiful art deco building and
former brewery turned huge arts centre.
It hosts very interesting exhibitions that
often focus on the interaction between
social issues and art as a communicative
space. Do you prefer liquid Berliner
KINDL? The on-site Café Babette has got
you covered!

5

MUSEUMS YOU SHOULDN'T MISS

---

361 SCHWULES MUSEUM (GAY MUSEUM)

Lützowstrasse 73
Tiergarten ⑧
+49 (0)30 6959 9050
schwulesmuseum.de

This impressive museum is probably one of the world's most significant institutions when it comes to archiving, researching and communicating the history and culture of LGBTIQ communities. Temporary exhibitions and events offer diverse views on lesbian, gay, trans, bisexual and queer biographies, themes and concepts in history, art and culture. Free guided tours.

362 MUSEUM DER DINGE (MUSEUM OF THINGS)

Oranienstrasse 25
Kreuzberg ②
+49 (0)30 9210 6311
museumderdinge.de

Design delight! The name of this museum is ambivalent, and is also meant to be. The 'things' we're speaking of are actually a collection (all 'Made in Germany' *natürlich*) of everyday objects, presented just as they are, without too much explanation. Like that, they tell us the history of the last century. Also interesting here is the comparison between East and West German design.

361 SCHWULES MUSEUM

363 MUSEUM BERGGRUEN
Schlossstrasse 1
Charlottenburg ⑨
+49 (0)30 2664 24242

The Museum Berggruen in front of the Charlottenburg Castle is the little brother of the Neue National Gallery. Expect to see works of Giacometti, Paul Klee or Matisse but also excellent temporary exhibitions. And while you're there, why not pop in the gorgeous Bröhan Museum on the other side of the road?

364 DESIGNPANOPTIKUM
Torstrasse 201
Mitte ①
+49 (0)157 7401 2991

The Designpanoptiktum is a surrealist museum of industrial objects with a carnival-like atmosphere. One step inside and you'll be immersed in Vlad's (the owner's) world; think retro-tech attached to body parts, medical equipment connected to common items from all kinds of past and future eras. If you're into steampunk, you will absolutely love this!

365 BUCHSTABEN-MUSEUM
Stadtbahnbogen 424
Tiergarten ⑧
+49 (0)177 4201 87
buchstabenmuseum.de

The goal of the Buchstabenmuseum (Museum of Letters) is to document and preserve letters, and it especially focuses on the presentations of three-dimensional signs and their histories. A one of a kind museum and one not to be missed. Book an individual guided tour for getting the most of your visit.

The 5 best
SUMMER FESTIVALS

---

366 PANKE PARCOURS
VARIOUS LOCATIONS
Wedding ⑩
+49 (0)30 4549 0838
pankeparcours.de

A very sweet, down-to-earth, and authentic little festival in an equally down-to-earth Wedding. I especially love the DJ sets on the rooftop terrace of the famous Sculplobe in the Böttgerstrasse *(sculplobe.com)*. The coffee and natural wines at Baldon on the ground floor of this amazing building are pretty good, too.

367 TORSTRASSEN FESTIVAL
VARIOUS LOCATIONS
Mitte ①
torstrassenfestival.de

In cooperation with venues, cafes, shops and bars in and around the Torstrasse and the Rosenthalerplatz, the team behind this very nice festival strives to offer a forum for current and relevant developments in Berlin's different music scenes. It's a must for locals, visitors and influencers. Every year in June.

368 FOREIGN AFFAIRS FESTIVAL
AT: HAUS DER BERLINER
FESTSPIELE
Schaperstrasse 24
Charlottenburg ⑨
+49 (0)30 2548 9100
berlinerfestspiele.de

This festival takes place every year in July in the wonderful venue of the Haus der Berliner Festspiele. It is an international festival for contemporary performing arts, and every year it explores a different topic or theme. It offers an often unique chance to see the work of the world's best choreographers on stage, like Alain Platel or William Kentridge, in a first class venue.

369 LESBIAN AND GAY CITY FESTIVAL
Schöneberg ⑦
stadtfest.berlin

Every mid-July the neighbourhood around the Nollendorfplatz turns pink. For one weekend, the streets here are transformed into Berlin's most popular party zone with colourful stage shows, food, drinks, and information booths. It's Europe's largest gay festival and for some people it's even more important than the Gay Pride.

370 FUSION FESTIVAL
Am Flugplatz 1
Rechlin
+49 (0)30 6098 4377
fusion-festival.de

This festival takes place every year in June, at a former military airport in Rechlin, a two hour drive from Berlin. For the duration of this festival, its attendees immerse themselves in an avant-gardistic parallel society, looking for a better world by celebrating different styles of music, theatre, performance and art.

5 *unusual*

BERLIN VENUES

---

371 SPIEGELSAAL / MIRROR HALL
AT: CLÄRCHENS BALLROOM
Auguststrasse 24
Mitte ①
+49 (0)30 6108 7662
claerchensball.haus

Clärchens Ballhaus is an immensely popular place with tourists and locals alike. But it does hide a secret, and that's its *Spiegelsaal* (mirror hall). It wasn't used for 60 years and bears all the traces of war and the passing of time. It's not always open to the public, but sometimes there are chamber music performances here: check the website.

372 PIERRE BOULEZ CONCERT HALL
Französische Str. 33-D
Mitte ①
+49 (0)30 4799 7411
boulezsaal.de

This non-traditional concert hall opened in March 2017 and is part of the Barenboim-Said-Akademie. It was designed by American architect Frank Gehry, a friend of both Daniel Barenboim and Pierre Boulez. The venue can be configured in different ways and the sensual, elliptical shape gives the guests an intimate feeling. Fabulous acoustics.

373 DEUTSCHE OPER BERLIN

Bismarckstrasse 35
Charlottenburg ⑨
+49 (0)30 3438 4343
deutscheoperberlin.de

The German Opera was designed by Fritz Bornemann in 1961, in an ultra modernist style. For some people the look of this building might be too cold, but you can't say it hasn't got style. The sound quality is superb here, and the same goes for the plays that are staged.

374 BAR JEDER VERNUNFT

Schaperstrasse 24
Charlottenburg ⑨
+49 (0)30 8831 582
bar-jeder-vernunft.de

Just near the house of the Berliner Festspiele lies the glamorous Bar jeder Vernunft, known as a venue for old-time cabaret, comedy and good food. The wonderful atmosphere and the fantastic glittering mirror tent make this place absolutely worth a visit.

375 EHEMALIGES STUMMFILMKINO DELPHI

Gustav-Adolf-Str. 2
Prenzlauer Berg ③
+49 (0)30 4004 8587
theater-im-delphi.de

Marlene Dietrich and Fritz Lang are known to have walked along this street with its many cinemas in the 1920s. The Delphi theatre was one of the biggest and miraculously survived WWII, the GDR and the post-wall madness. It's one of the finest remaining witnesses of the glamour and flair of the heyday of German silent film. It's now used as a location for events.

The 5 best

ALTERNATIVE CINEMAS

---

376 **LICHTBLICK-KINO**
   Kastanienallee 77
   Prenzlauer Berg ③
   +49 (0)30 4405 8179
   lichtblick-kino.org

Nice small theatre with a seedy, very Berlin-like, look from the outside, that seats only 32 people. The programming focuses on independent art house movies and documentaries in their original version, with German subtitles.

377 **KINO CENTRAL**
   Rosenthaler Str. 39
   Mitte ①
   +49 (0)30 2859 9973
   kino-central.de

Kino Central is an independent cinema in the courtyard of Haus Schwartzenberg. In summer you can enjoy a movie in the open air. The atmosphere is very 1990s, and the programming is eclectic, with also lots of good children's movies.

378 **BABYLON**
   Rosa-Luxemburg-Strasse 30
   Mitte ①
   +49 (0)30 2425 969
   babylonberlin.de

This theatre was built in 1929 in an art deco style and survived the war. The programming is absolutely first class, but the real pride and joy of this place is the restored cinema organ, dating from 1929. Check the website for screenings with organ accompaniment.

379 **MOVIEMIENTO**
Kottbusser Damm 22
Kreuzberg ②
+49 (0)30 6924 785
moviemento.de

Germany's oldest cinema has three auditoria and a lounge. You can see art house films here but also more mainstream stuff, and some pretty nice children's films. Some films are dubbed in German, so check the website.

380 **KINO INTERNATIONAL**
Karl-Marx-Allee 33
Mitte ①
+49 (0)30 2475 6011
kino-international.com

Kino International was the GDR's premier cinema and still is a real architectural highlight. It is also one of the very rare cinemas that still display hand-illustrated film posters.

380 KINO INTERNATIONAL

5 places where you might find
GOOD BUSKERS

---

381 **ALEXANDERPLATZ**
 Mitte ①

At first sight, the Alexanderplatz looks like a consumers' paradise with shops everywhere, but it does have the beauty of brutalist architecture. The Alexanderplatz is popular with street artists, and if you're lucky, you can enjoy performances by talented musicians (like Charity Children) in front of the Saturn shop or under the trainrails.

382 MAUERPARK

382 MAUERPARK
Prenzlauer Berg ③

Here's the only park in Berlin where musicians can play amplified music without having to have a permit. You can find really good street musicians here, like Teresa Bergman, Alice Phoebe Lou, or Charity Children, just to name a few. Don't miss the karaoke on hot summer Sundays!

383 HACKESCHER MARKT
Mitte ①

The always-crowded Hackescher Markt is a good place to hear some good street musicians. You could bump into a German funk band (yes, German can be funky!), a klezmer band, or a Balkan blues band.

384 PRINZESSINNEN-GÄRTEN
Prinzenstrasse 35 / Moritzplatz
Kreuzberg ②
prinzessinnengarten.net

Every second Sunday in summer, a nice flea market takes place at the Prinzessinnengarten. There are often very talented musicians here, who have the privilege of having a real podium and sound system at their disposal.

385 WARSCHAUER STRASSE
Friedrichshain ④

The people who are performing on the Warschauer Bridge and in front of the underground-station are pretty courageous. On some days, a big crowd will gather around a particularly good street musician, on other days, it's the opposite.

5 places to enjoy culture if you
DON'T SPEAK GERMAN

---

386 **F40 ENGLISH THEATRE**
Fidicinstrasse 40
Kreuzberg ②
+49 (0)30 6911 211
etberlin.de

F40 features three or four English Theatre Berlin productions a month, by local and international talents. There's a year-round programming which comprises the in-house productions, selected international productions and work from Berlin's independent performing arts community, as well as concerts and comedy and drama education.

387 **SCHAUBÜHNE**
Kurfürstendamm 153
Charlottenburg ⑨
+49 (0)30 8900 23
schaubuehne.de

The Schaubühne is a famous Berlin theatre in West Berlin. Since 1999, it has been under the wings of artistic director Thomas Ostermeier, who made his ensemble an international success. One of the theatre's distinctive features is a stylistic variety in approaches to directing, including new forms of dance and musical theatre. Resident star actors are Lars Eidinger and Nina Hoss.

388 HAU

HAU1:
Stresemannstr. 29
HAU2: Hallesches
Ufer 32
HAU3: Tempelhofer
Ufer 10
Kreuzberg ②
+49 (0)30 2590 0427
hebbel-am-ufer.de

Hau was founded after the fusion of three theatres in the same neighbourhood. It is a theatre and international performance centre with a rather edgy image. Since 2004 HAU stands for the best, most experimental international programme the city has to offer, with a bold blend of contemporary dance and multimedia performances.

389 MAXIM GORKI THEATRE

Am Festungsgraben 2
Mitte ①
+49 (0)30 2022 1115
gorki.de

The Maxim Gorki Theatre, named after the Russian writer Gorky and located in the Choral Academy on the boulevard Unter den Linden, is the smallest and most beautiful of Berlin's ensemble theatres. Through their eclectic programming and strong image they invite us to think about the human condition and the conflict of identity.

390 RADIALSYSTEM V

Holzmarktstrasse 33
Friedrichshain ④
+49 (0)30 2887 88588
radialsystem.de

This fantastic venue is housed in a former sewage pumping station on the river Spree, and offers a programme that goes way beyond traditional concerts, dance and theatre performances. Radialsystem V continually develops new and innovative ideas and also regularly has educational workshops for children and teenagers in the field of music and dance.

5 *important*
CULTURAL FESTIVALS

391 BERLINALE
FEBRUARY
berlinale.de

The Berlinale must be Berlin's most famous festival. It's one of the most important dates for the international film industry: more than 335.000 tickets are sold every year, and there are more than 20.000 professional visitors from 122 countries. That's a lot of glitter and glamour for 'poor but sexy' Berlin. Buy your tickets early!

**392 TANZ IM AUGUST /
DANCE IN AUGUST**
AUGUST / SEPTEMBER
+49 (0)30 2590 0427
tanzimaugust.de

Germany's biggest festival for contemporary dance began as an avant-garde and experimental festival. During later years, it moved on to being about more than niche art, and it now stands for great guest performances. The festival (presented by HAU) explores the link between visual art and movement.

393 48 STUNDEN NEUKÖLLN
END OF JUNE
Neukölln
48-stunden-neukoelln.de

Two days of art in Berlin's hippest district. The festival is a joint initiative involving artists, spectators and other residents. The organisers try to involve all segments of the local population, regardless of age, ethnic background or social standing. Bringing art closer to the people, it had been tried before, but 48 Stunden Neukölln really seems to succeed in its mission.

394 BERLIN BIENNALE FOR CONTEMPORARY ART
EVERY EVEN YEAR ON DIFFERENT LOCATIONS
blog.berlinbiennale.de

The Berlin Biennale has established itself as an 'open space' that experiments with, identifies and critically examines the latest trends in the world of art. This 'art lab' has a strong focus on the post-contemporary condition. Don't expect too many established names. The latest editions are proving to be a polarising affair.

395 INTERNATIONALES LITERATURFESTIVAL BERLIN
SEPTEMBER
Chausseestrasse 5
Mitte ①
+49 (0)30 2787 8620
literaturfestival.com

The Berlin International Literature Festival invites contemporary authors of prose and poetry from all over the world to present their work in the original language. The texts, poems and verses are grouped thematically into five sections: literatures of the world, reflections, international children's and young adult literature, 'Speak, Memory' as well as specials.

PARK AM GLEISDREIECK

25 THINGS TO DO
WITH CHILDREN

The 5 best
PLAYGROUNDS

---

396 BRITZER GARTEN

Sangerhauser Weg 1
Neukölln ⑥
+49 (0)30 7009 0680
gruen-berlin.de/
britzer-garten

This is one of the 5 best of the 1850 playgrounds in Berlin. Not because of specific playground equipment but because it covers 90 hectares of playgrounds, lakes and hills, and other buildings where you can explore nature and reconnect with it.

397 WITCH PLAYGROUND

Eisenacher Strasse 29
Schöneberg ⑦

Here you'll find 3000 m² of play fun, featuring a teetering tower without safety net, a long, dramatic zipline and a huge wooden pirate ship with rope bridges. But the real highlight is the two-storey high witchhouse.

398 PLÄNTERWALD

Treptow-Köpenick ⑤
pro-plaenterwald.de

Check out Berlin's biggest water playground in this huge forest. It's not exactly posh and modern but kids just love it! There's even an ice-cream truck on site. In the *Waldspielplatz* (forest playground) kids can build their own tree house.

399 PARK AM GLEISDREIECK

Möckernstrasse 26
Kreuzberg ②
+49 (0)30 7009 060
*gruen-berlin.de/
gleisdreieck*

This park is a reconverted former train yard, which seems to expand every year. It's often criticised for being too postmodern but we think it's absolutely gorgeous in every way: it's huge and green and it appeals to all ages. You might go there for the many beach volleyball courts, or for the different playgrounds, or for the skate park.

400 WALDHOCHSEIL-GARTEN JUNGFERNHEIDE

Heckerdamm 260
Charlottenburg ⑨
+49 (0)30 3409 4818
*waldhochseilgarten-
jungfernheide.de*

This is a climbing forest worthy of Robinson Crusoe. Children from the age of 6 onwards (and adults!) are strapped into harnesses and then get to play on a network of ziplines and balance beams stretched high up in the trees. Open daily, from March through October.

399 PARK AM GLEISDREIECK

5 places to
COOL DOWN
IN SUMMER

---

401 SOMMERBAD PANKOW

Wolfshagener
Strasse 91-93
Pankow
+49 (0)30 2219 0011
*berlinerbaeder.de/
baeder/sommerbad-
pankow*

Berlin has a huge amount of indoor and outdoor pools. Summers in Berlin are nice and sunny and it's great to spend a day at an outdoor pool. The Sommerbad in Pankow is surrounded by a big leafy park. Young kids will love the slides, older kids will prefer the diving tower.

403 STRANDBAD WANNSEE

402 STADTBAD MITTE 'JAMES SIMON'

Gartenstrasse 5
Mitte ①
+49 (0)30 2219 0011
berlinerbaeder.de/
baeder/stadtbad-mitte

If the sun isn't shining, you can always take the kids to have a swim in one of Berlin's many indoor pools. The Stadtbad Mitte for example, is a genuine architectural gem that opened in 1929. It has an all-glass facade and the water temperature is always a pleasant 27,5°C.

403 STRANDBAD WANNSEE

Wannseebadweg 25
Nikolassee
+49 (0)30 2219 0011
berlinerbaeder.de/
baeder/strandbad-
wannsee

Take the S-Bahn to Wannsee and you'll soon arrive in summer heaven, more precisely the big open-air lido at the beautiful Wannsee lake. This beach has been around for more than 100 years already. In summertime it's open from 8 am to 9 pm. Naked bathing is allowed.

404 KINDERBAD MONBIJOU

Oranienburger
Strasse 78
Mitte ①
+49 (0)30 2219 0011
berlinerbaeder.de/
baeder/kinderbad-
monbijou

This is probably one of the smallest pools in the city, but the location in the middle of the Monbijou park, with a view on the Museum Island, is so fantastic, one cannot afford not to mention it. The kids can play in the pool and their parents can lie down on the grass and plan their next trip to Berlin.

405 FREIBAD PLÖTZENSEE

Nordufer 26
Wedding ⑩
+49 (0)30 8964 4787
strandbad-
ploetzensee.de

This beautiful little lake has a particularly old-school charm that many other beach areas around Berlin lack. There's a dedicated FKK (nudist) beach. You can get a massage in the sweet pagoda on the beach or go clubbing in the brand-new Plötze. If you just want a beer, go to the Fischerpinte, a picturesque boathouse on the other side of the lake.

5 *excellent*
ICE-CREAM VENDORS

406 WOOP WOOP ICE CREAM

Rosenthaler Str. 3
+ Foodtruck
Mitte ①
+49 (0)176 7214 9575
woopwoopicecream.de

You might find this food truck at Bite Club, at Markthalle Neun or at Checkpoint Charlie. Owners Philipp and Boris (aka the cream team) produce their fresh ice cream using liquid nitrogen at a temperature close to -200°C.

407 CUORE DI VETRO

Max-Beer-Strasse 33
Mitte ①
cuoredivetro.berlin

Cuore di Vetro is not only a very good ice-cream parlour but also a place where spontaneous concerts or exhibitions can happen. Everything is made in house in true Italian style. Some say they have the best dark chocolate ice cream in Berlin. Try their Affogato, an espresso poured over a scoop of vanilla ice cream.

408 ESMERALDA'S INKA-CAFÉ

Belziger Strasse 44
Schöneberg ⑦
+49 (0)163 7025 734

This South-American themed ice-cream shop has many flavours on offer, like custard apple, tamarind, purple corn, and grainy *lúcuma*. If you don't feel like ice cream, the menu also includes *empanadas* or other (mainly Peruvian) snacks.

409 JONES ICE CREAM

Goltzstrasse 3
Schöneberg ⑦
+49 (0)171 8335 780
jonesicecream.com

Is it because of the delicious handmade cookie-cones – soft on the inside, crunchy on the outside? Or is it because of the myriad of fresh ice-cream flavours like pineapple-ginger? Whatever the reason, this place will convince you that an ice-cream cone is the answer to all your problems.

410 EISBOX

Elberfelder Str. 27
Tiergarten ⑧
Moabit
+49 (0)30 5448 4652
eisbox.eu

This place might seem a bit far off track, and it isn't cheap, but we can ensure you that the quality and the taste of the flavours are worth it. Everything is organic, no additions or artificial flavours allowed. This means that the flavours change daily, depending on the freshness and availability of ingredients. Try their saffron with orange blossom flavour.

406 WOOP WOOP ICE CREAM

5

CHILD-FRIENDLY MUSEUMS

---

411 **JUGEND MUSEUM SCHÖNEBERG**

Hauptstrasse 40-42
Schöneberg ①
+49 0(30) 9027 76163
jugendmuseum.de

This 'Youth Museum' is housed in the so-called Million Dollar Villa. It was conceived as a place that encourages experimentation and curiosity. There are two permanent expositions but the museum also offers temporary expos and workshops. It's ideal for children from 8 years onwards.

412 **PUPPENTHEATER MUSEUM**

Karl-Marx-Strasse 135
Neukölln ①
+49 (0)30 6878 132
puppentheater-museum.de

The Karl-Marx-Strasse is not exactly touristy and it's not exactly pretty, but there are so many hidden gems to be discovered behind its dingy façade that would be a pity to overlook. The Puppet Theatre Museum is one of them. You will enter the phantasy world of different kinds of marionettes and puppets from all over the world.

413 MACHMIT!

Senefelderstrasse 5-6
Prenzlauer Berg ③
+49 (0)30 7477 8200
machmitmuseum.de

This is a very special children's museum located in a converted church, the former Eliaskirche. It encourages its visitors to participate and get active. Workshops, experiential exhibitions, a printing shop and a nice cafe make this place really worth the trip. For children from 4 to 12.

414 LABYRINTH KINDERMUSEUM

Osloerstrasse 12
Mitte ③
+49 (0)30 8009 31150
labyrinth-kindermuseum.de

'Learning by doing' is the motto of this museum, housed in a former factory in the Wedding district. The interactive exhibitions have many different themes, from fairy tales to children's rights, and they give your children the opportunity to gain knowledge while playing. For children aged 3 to 12.

415 KIDS GALLERY IN THE BODE-MUSEUM

Am Kupfergraben
Mitte ①
+49 (0)30 2664 24242
smb.museum

Not many people know that the Bode-Museum, specialised in Byzantine art, also has an interesting children's gallery and a very nice bar. After your visit, you can go out and enjoy listening to the buskers on the bridge or, if you're there on a Saturday or a Sunday, go find hidden treasures at the antiques and book market along the riverside.

5 shops and bars where
KIDS ARE WELCOME

416 **EMMA & PAUL FAMILIENCAFÉ**

Gleditschstrasse 47
Schöneberg ⑧
+49 (0)30 2362 8368
emma-pauls-
biergarten.com

Children from 0 to 6 are more than welcome in this family cafe that is especially popular for its Saturday and Sunday brunches. While the parents are socialising in the cafe, the kids are having the time of their lives in the playroom; definitely a win-win situation.

417 **CHARLOTTCHEN**

Droysenstrasse 1
Charlottenburg ⑨
+49 (0)30 3244 717
restaurant-
charlottchen.de

'Little Charlotte' is a theatre and also a family restaurant that has been around since 1990. On their programme they have a colourful range of events for children including magic shows, clowns, and traditional puppet theatre shows.
The restaurant is also worth a visit in itself. After dinner, kids can go to the giant playroom while the parents can continue to enjoy their meal, without stress.

418 FANTASIA

Danckelmannstr. 10
Charlottenburg ⑨
+49 (0)30 3248 668
fantasia-spielzeug.de

A shop full of consoles, computer games, CD-ROMs and role-playing games but also lots of Lego and a selection of second-hand toys and board games as well as an exchange service. If you want to keep your kids from doing their homework for a couple of weeks, you should bring them here.

419 ONKEL PHILIPP'S SPIELZEUG-WERKSTATT

Choriner Strasse 35
Prenzlauer Berg ③
+49 (0)30 4490 491
onkel-philipp.de

This is a kind of hidden toy museum, with a vast collection of GDR-era toys packed in the cellar. It's a bit weird and surprising to see toys piled up in a basement like this and we're not sure that every kid would love it, but the toyshop and repair service are certainly two of the district's favourite spots for kids.

420 J-STORE

Kantstrasse 125
Charlottenburg ⑨
+49 (0)30 3180 1400
j-store-berlin.de

J-Store is a mini-emporium devoted to manga/anime. It's one of only two addresses in Germany with a so-called 'My Purikura' photobooth. While the kids get high on the *kawaii* cuteness overload, parents can sneak off to the nearby cafe of the Japanese bakery Kame for a delicious *matcha* cheesecake.

HÜTTENPALAST

20 PLACES TO SLEEP LIKE A BABY

5

HIPPER THAN HIP HOTELS

---

421 MICHELBERGER HOTEL

Warschauer Str. 39-40
Friedrichshain ④
+49 (0)30 2977 8590
www.michelberger
hotel.com

The main clientele of this eco shabby chic hotel consists of models, artists and media people as well as techno-clubbers. Check their Facebook-page for pop-up-concerts by stars like Damien Rice or Arcade Fire. Most of the rooms in this budget boutique hotel are very small.

422 25HOURS HOTEL BIKINI BERLIN

Budapester Str. 40
Tiergarten ⑧
+49 (0)30 1202 210
www.25hours-
hotels.com

Former West Berlin was never considered really trendy, but that has started to change with the opening of the Bikini shopping mall and the 25hours Hotel Bikini. The rooms in the hotel are very modern and glossy and all have huge windows so you can enjoy the great view on the zoo.

423 SOHO HOUSE BERLIN

Torstrasse 1
Mitte ①
+49 (0)30 4050 440
www.sohohouse
berlin.com

Soho House is the favourite hotel of the rich and famous. From the Soho shop to the rooftop terrace (8 floors), everything in this New Objectivity building is redolent of creativity, art and design. Just don't forget that you need to be a member to book a room.

424 HÜTTENPALAST

Hobrechtstr. 65-66
Neukölln ⑥
+49 (0)30 3730 5806
www.huettenpalast.de

An urban camping, that's maybe the best way to describe this unique hotel installed in a former vacuum factory. The old warehouse offers plenty of space for a number of caravans and wooden cabins that all have been beautifully decorated by the owners Silke and Sarah.

425 ALMODÓVAR

Boxhagener Str. 83
Friedrichshain ④
+49 (0)30 6920 97080
www.almodovarhotel.de

This beautiful design hotel was named after the extravagant Spanish film director. It's Berlin's first vegetarian organic hotel; its restaurant Bistro Bardot is also open to non-guests. All rooms have yoga mats, TV and Internet.

424 HÜTTENPALAST

The 5 best

CHEAP HO(S)TELS

426 THE CIRCUS HOSTEL

Weinbergsweg 1-A
Mitte ①
+49 (0)30 2000 3939
circus-berlin.de

The Circus Hostel is not only cheap but also nicely designed and it offers good and professional service. There are a few private single rooms for guests who don't like sleeping in a dormitory. They also have an in-house bar, a cafe and even their own brewery. If you're looking for a bit more luxury book a room at The Circus Hotel (without the 's') on the other side of the Rosenthaler Platz.

427 GENERATOR

Oranienburgerstr. 65
Mitte ①
+49 (0)30 9210 37680
generatorhostels.com

The Oranienburgerstrasse used to be the heart of the alternative Mitte district but these days it's rather difficult to find a bar or restaurant with a heart here. Fortunately there are still some exceptions like the shabby X-terrain bar or the little Thai restaurant called Kamala. The Generator itself is a very well designed hostel that offers all modern facilities.

428 GRAND HOSTEL

Tempelhofer Ufer 14
Kreuzberg ②
+49 (0)30 2009 5450
grandhostel-berlin.de

Grand Hostel has two branches in Berlin: the classic branch, with cosy rooms in a historic building in Kreuzberg and the urban one, a hostel in trendy Neukölln. The latter has a more Eastern European vibe to it although both hostels are situated in former West Berlin. They also organise bar- and city bike tours.

429 PENSION 11HIMMEL

Wittenberger Str. 85
Marzahn
+49 (0)30 9377 2052
pension-11himmel.de

Marzahn is traditionally a poor district in former East Berlin and has a lot of *Plattenbau*: the German term for the concrete prefab apartments that were built under the communist regime. It's still an absolutely non-hip but therefore also authentic part of Berlin. The pension has a lot in common with the Ostel but it's more genuine and a lot smaller. The owners claim to give you the 'total Plattenbau experience' during your stay.

430 SINGER109

Singerstrasse 109
Friedrichshain ④
+49 (0)30 7477 5028
singer109.com

This hostel in itself isn't very special but it has a very nice atrium and a perfect location if you like to go out dancing in clubs like Yaam, Kater Blau or others near the river Spree in Friedrichshain: it's so close by you can crawl back to your dorm if the night was a little bit too heavy.

The 5 most
UNUSUAL PLACES
to sleep

---

431 PROVOCATEUR

Brandenburgische
Strasse 21
Charlottenburg ⑨
+49 (0)30 2205 6060
provocateur-hotel.com

Hotel Provocateur is a design hotel near the Schaubühne in West-Berlin. If you love great design and luxury and don't mind a bit of provocation here and there, then this is the place to be.

432 NHOW BERLIN

Stralauer Allee 3
Friedrichshain ④
+49 (0)30 2902 990
nh-hotels.de/hotel/
nhow-berlin

This huge hotel was built near the Universal building on the so-called Media Spree – on this bank of the Spree several media-players have their offices. Nhow attracts a lot of musicians, not only because of the radical design of the hotel by architect Karim Rashid but also because of the in-house concerts and fashion shows. All 304 rooms have stunning views.

433 HOTEL ZOO

Kurfürstendamm 25
Charlottenburg ⑨
+49 (0)30 884 370
hotelzoo.de

A big hotel (141 rooms) in the heart of former West Berlin is not something we normally would include in this list. But this hotel stands out by the combination of pre-war nostalgia combined with great design and art. The building itself is over 120 years old. Tip: also non-guests can have a beer at the rooftop bar, a real gem!

434 MODERN HOUSEBOAT
ON LAKE RUMMELSBURG
Lichtenberg
+49 (0)163 7372 509
modernhouseboat.com

This private (boat) house lies in a little working harbour on the river Spree, namely in Rummelsburg, and offers a truly wonderful view on the water. It's only 10 minutes by car or tram to the funky district of Friedrichshain. The building features modern design, large windows and a fireplace.

435 HOTEL-PENSION FUNK
Fasanenstrasse 69
Charlottenburg ⑨
+49 (0)30 8827 193
hotel-pensionfunk.de

Built in 1895, this house reached fame through its prominent inhabitant, the world famous actress of silent movies Asta Nielsen. The hotel is pretty authentic and the detailed art nouveau windows and beautiful ceilings are well preserved. Ideal if you like small, well priced hotels with a lot of character.

435 HOTEL-PENSION FUNK

The 5 best
BOUTIQUE HOTELS

---

436 DAS STUE

Drakestrasse 1
Tiergarten ⑧
+49 (0)30 3117 220
das-stue.com

If you're a design lover and you're looking for a place to stay that's comfortable and easy-going, and if you can afford a stay at Das Stue, then look no further: this is your dream hotel. Everything is just perfect here, from the elegant restaurant Cinco, which was awarded a Michelin star within a year after opening (thanks to Catalan master chef Paco Pérez), over the wonderful rooms, to the free access to the zoo.

437 ACKSELHAUS & BLUE HOME

Belforter Strasse 21
Prenzlauer Berg ③
+49 (0)30 4433 7633
ackselhaus.de

Two hotels in one! The Ackselhaus offers mainly apartments while the (more pricey) Blue Home offers the typical hotel services. Outside there is the rumble of the urban jungle, inside the beautiful Mediterranean-inspired garden behind the 120-year-old restored building provides a place of calm for the guests. The Club del Mar cafe serves an excellent breakfast.

438 SCHLOSSHOTEL BERLIN

Brahmsstrasse 10
Grunewald
+49 (0)30 8958 430
schlosshotelberlin.com

Fashion designer Patrick Hellman bought this hotel in 2014. He wanted to keep the charm of the rooms – after all they were redesigned by Karl Lagerfeld in the nineties – but also give the hotel a more contemporary touch. It's now an oasis of luxury and good taste. Don't miss the cigar lounge with the fireplace.

439 THE MANDALA HOTEL

Potsdamer Strasse 3
Mitte ①
+49 (0)30 5900 50000
themandala.de

Despite being part of a large chain, the Mandala Hotel has enough character to make its guests fall in love. Its location on the Potzdamer Platz is as central as can be: this is where the Wall once stood, right in the middle of former West and East Berlin. The rooms are pleasant and functional and the restaurant Facil has two Michelin stars.

440 THE DUDE

Köpenicker Strasse 92
Mitte ①
+49 (0)30 4119 88177
thedudeberlin.com

This small and privately owned luxurious boutique hotel is located in a lovely nineteenth-century townhouse on the busy Köpenicker Strasse. It has both a very posh and a very warm, personal feeling to it. We like the hip room amenities like the Moleskine notebooks and the Molton Brown toiletries. The in-house steak restaurant is called the Brooklyn Beef Club.

FREISCHWIMMER

25 DIFFERENT WAYS TO SPEND THE WEEKEND IN BERLIN

5 awesome
BIKING TOURS

---

441 ALONG THE OLD BERLIN WALL
Mauer-Radweg

The Mauer-Radweg follows the former wall's entire winding route – all 174 kilometres of it. You can cycle the entire track in one go, or you can decide to stop overnight along the way. The trail is signposted and divided into sections; you can reach each starting point by train or underground. If you are a short-term visitor, maybe it's wise to opt for a half-day tour; many guides offer them.

442 AROUND THE GRUNEWALD (GREEN FOREST) IN THE WEST

Take the train up to the S-Bahnhof Grunewald, and look for the signs. Your pleasant bike ride through the shadowy forest will also take you to the *Teufelssee* (the lake of the devil) and the historical landmark of the Grunewald Turm (tower). If you're brave enough to climb it, you'll be rewarded with a splendid view.

443 AROUND MÜGGELSEE FOR SOME VINTAGE GDR

The big and the small Müggelsee in the East of Berlin are a perfect destination for an easy bike trip. Take the S-Bahn (take your bike with you on the train or rent one when you're there) to Friedrichshagen. You'll pass by plenty of beer gardens and ice-cream parlours along the way. Have dinner in the amazing former GDR restaurant-tower called the Müggelturm.

444 ALL THE WAY TO COPENHAGEN

bike-berlin-copenhagen.com

In 2010 the city of Berlin completed its bucolic, riverside stretch of the 671-kilometre-long bike trail between Berlin and Copenhagen. This isn't exactly a weekend trip, so better plan ahead. The trail is divided in three stages: the Brandenburger stage (about 150 km), the Mecklenburger stage (250 km) and the Denmark stage (300 km).

445 AROUND BRANDENBURG

brandenburg-tourism.com/discover-brandenburg/brandenburg-by-bike.html

The beautiful, rural State of Brandenburg can easily be reached by car or public transport. No less than 7000 kilometres of newly built cycle paths (and they're mostly flat) will lead you to the State's key nature attractions. The website 'Brandenburg by Bike' will suggest several ready-made bike tours to choose from.

5 great
PICNIC SPOTS

---

446 **THAI PARK**
    AT: PREUSSENPARK
    **Brandenburgische
    Strasse
    Charlottenburg** ⑨

Forget expensive trips to Thailand: here's Thai street food at its best! Every weekend, at the so called *Thai Wiese* (Thai Meadow) in the Preussenpark, local Thais sell their homemade food. You'll enjoy the unique Asian atmosphere and maybe papaya salad to die for.

447 **VOLKSPARK
    FRIEDRICHSHAIN**
    **Am Friedrichshain 1
    Friedrichshain /
    Prenzlauer Berg** ③

This is Berlin's oldest municipal park. Part of it was destroyed by Allied bombs during the war. The hill in the park remains a witness to those events: it's called Mont Klamott (Clothing Hill, 78 metres) and is made of rubble from the ruins of destroyed Nazi bunkers.

448 **THE ISLAND OF YOUTH
    (INSEL DER JUGEND)**
    AT: TREPTOWER PARK
    **Alt-Treptow 6
    Alt-Treptow** ⑤
    +49 (0)30 8096 1850
    inselberlin.de

This island in the middle of the Spree river lies in beautiful Treptower Park and you can only get there by crossing a small, romantic bridge. There's also a charming restaurant and bar on the island if you don't like to bring your own food. In the garden you can rent vintage canoes and small boats – look for the 'Kanuliebe' sign.

449 TEMPELHOFER FELD
Neukölln ⑥

After a referendum was held, it became clear that the people of Berlin weren't going to hand over Tempelhof Field Airport – famous for its role during the Nazi regime and the famous airlift of 1948-1949 – to developers. Now, it's Berlin's second largest park. If you're not into landkiting, walking or biking, book a tour at the Airport Building: Tempelhof Airport Visit, Platz der Luftbrücke 5.

450 KÖRNERPARK
Schierker Strasse 8
Neukölln ①
+49 (0)30 5682 3939
körnerpark.de

This rather small park doesn't have that typical edgy Neukölln feeling; instead it's super neat and also perfect for a romantic picnic. The small cafe located inside the park rents out picnic baskets and during summer there are also free concerts, every Sunday at 6 pm.

450 KÖRNERPARK

The 5 most
BEAUTIFUL LAKES
around Berlin

---

451 **GROSS GLIENICKER SEE**
Potsdam

This lake is a little bit further away from the city but it's absolutely worth the trip, not only because of the extremely clear water, but also because of the two little green islands. There are two sandy beaches and there's a bus stop near the lake.

455 LIETZENSEE

452 SCHLACHTENSEE
Steglitz-Zehlendorf

This is one of the most beautiful lakes that public transportation will ever take you to. The Schlachtensee, on the border of the Grünewald, is rated Berlin's cleanest lake. It's a pristine spot for swimming as well as an ideal hiking area. Go to the Fischer Hütte for a cold post-swim beer.

453 MÜGGELSEE
Treptow-Köpenick ⑤
spreearche.de

Berlin's largest lake, east of Köpenick, is fed by the Spree. The lower section of the lake – the Kleiner Müggelsee – is perfect for swimming and a chill-out afternoon. The big Müggelsee is perfect for a boat trip – there are boats for rent. A perfect place for dinner is the Spreearche, a log-house that you can only reach by mini-ferry.

454 SACROWER SEE
Potsdam

This less frequented but clean and beautiful lake is a bit more difficult to reach. There's only one real beach at the lake, next to the restaurant Landleben Potsdam.

455 LIETZENSEE
Charlottenburg ⑨

The large Lietzensee can get pretty crowded because of its proximity to the city, but still it's absolutely worth a visit. The Parkhaus Lietzensee is stunning and sells ice cream on sunny afternoons.

The 5 most stunning
WELLNESS SPOTS

---

456 SURYA VILLA

Rykestrasse 3
Prenzlauer Berg ③
+49 (0)30 4849 5780
*ayurveda-wellness
zentrum.de*

This part of gentrified former East Berlin with its leafy cobbled streets is very enjoyable. The treatments at Surya Villa wellness centre are based on traditional Ayurveda medicine. Whether you want a massage or to find out your Ayurvedic type, their professional team will take good care of you.

457 VABALI

Seydlitzstrasse 6
Mitte ①
+49 (0)30 9114 860
vabali.de

After just one minute inside this textile-free spa you'll forget all about the city around you. Eleven saunas, different pools and places to rest, lots of waterbeds in darkened rooms and massage opportunities will keep you busy or, better, zen, all day.

458 HOTEL STADTBAD ODERBERGER

Oderberger Strasse 57
Prenzlauer Berg ③
+49 (0)30 7800 89760
hotel-oderberger.berlin

The *Mietskasernen* (tenements) built during the Grunderzeit didn't have private bathrooms. As the population in Berlin was booming around 1900, the need for public bathhouses grew. Stadbadt Oderberger opened in 1902. It was turned into a hotel in 2016. The pool and sauna are stunning, as is the rest of this boutique hotel.

459 LIQUIDROM

Möckernstrasse 10
Kreuzberg ②
+49 (0)30 2580 07820
liquidrom-berlin.de

Liquidrom has four saunas or you can also have a massage or chill out in the inner courtyard with its small salt pool. The real highlight is the darkened salt water pool in a dimmed upola hall with oceanic music.

460 HAMAM

AT: FRAUENZENTRUM
SCHOKOLADENFABRIK
Mariannenstrasse 6
Kreuzberg ②
+49 (0)30 6151 464
hamamberlin.de

This small hammam is part of the Schokoladenfabrik, a Women's Centre in Berlin. Located in a former chocolate factory, it opened in 1988 as the first hammam in Germany. The hammam not only cleanses your body and soul but it's also a meeting point for women of different cultures and ages. Women only.

459 LIQUIDROM

5 unusual venues with a
LAKE or RIVER VIEW

---

461 SEEBAD FRIEDRICHSHAGEN

Müggelseedamm 216
Treptow-Köpenick ⑤
+49 (0)30 6455 756
*seebadfriedrichs
hagen.de*

The view from this beach on the Müggelsee is simply amazing. Dive from the broad wooden pier that leads out into the lake and swim back to the beach to sip a margarita in one of the many deck chairs. There's a rental service with various boats and rafts.

462 BOOTSHAUS STELLA AM LIETZENSEE

Witzlebenplatz 1A
Charlottenburg ⑨
+49 (0)30 3012 7781
*bootshaus
amlietzensee.de*

Charlottenburg is probably the only neighbourhood in Berlin with a certain Parisian grandeur. It also has a very beautiful lake situated in the Lietzenseepark where you can easily spend the day and where the noises of the nearby city are shut out. If you get thirsty, there's a beautiful boathouse/beer garden on the banks of the Lietzensee with a huge terrace built on pillars. Prost!

463 ANKLERKLAUSE

Kottbusser Damm 104
Kreuzberg ②
+49 (0)30 6935 649
ankerklause.de

This former boathouse has a genuine maritime feeling to it. The decor is kitschy and cosy and the restaurant and bar are perched over the Spree river canal near the open-air Türkenmarkt. The sundown on both of the patios is beautiful.

464 YAAM

An Der
Schillingbrücke 3
Friedrichshain ④
+49 (0)30 6151 354
yaam.de

Yaam (short for the Young and African Arts Market) is a bit of an atypical beach club. It's a club, a beach bar (one of the oldest in Berlin) and a concert venue (focussing on reggae and world music) as well. It's the perfect multiculti chill-out location.

465 FREISCHWIMMER

Vor dem
Schlesischen Tor 2-A
Friedrichshain ④
+49 (0)30 6107 4309
freischwimmer-berlin.com/

This former boat rental with repair shop was transformed into a hip restaurant. It offers a fantastic view on the water and on the Arena buildings on the other side of the river. Despite the fact that it isn't easy to find (a tip: it's just 100 metres behind the ARAL petrol station), it's very popular. It's the perfect location for a Sunday brunch.

463 ANKERKLAUSE

KREUZBERG

35 RANDOM FACTS AND URBAN DETAILS

---

5 funky
BERLIN BLOGS
in English

---

466 CEE CEE

ceecee.cc

Cee Cee was launched in 2011 as a newsletter for friends but now it's Berlin's most widely read online medium. The blog always has its finger on the pulse when it comes to Berlin's rich cultural and lifestyle scene. If you want to know about the latest hotspots in the city, this is the site you're looking for.

467 ASK HELMUT

askhelmut.com/berlin

Helmut was born in Berlin but has since then expanded his work area to six major cities. Ask Helmut for everything you always wanted to know about performing arts. The website is easy to use and always up-to-date. He speaks English and German. Great guy, that Helmut.

468 DIGITAL COSMONAUT

digitalcosmonaut.com

Excellent blog by @iamkosmonaut who is passionate about urbexing, trains and post-war Berlin. If you want to know where to find the last depictions of Karl Marx in Berlin or why that particular train station has a frog king statue, you came to the right place.

469 THE NEEDLE

needleberlin.com

'The needle' is the omnipresent Fernsehturm (TV-tower) on Alexander-platz and Berlin's best-known landmark, but the name of this blog also refers to the sharp eye of its writer, historian Joseph Pearson. This is the perfect resource when you're looking for in-depth posts on the history of Berlin and it also pays a lot of attention to what's going on in Berlin's culture scene. (The focus is on theatre since Pearson is also and essayist and blogger for the Schaubühne Theatre).

470 STIL IN BERLIN

stilinberlin.de

This blog is mainly the work of Mary Sherpe. A decade ago it was completely dedicated to street style in Berlin but its scope is now broader, also covering food, art, and lifestyle in general. Thanks to Sherpe's beautiful photos and her easy-to-read writing style her blog has become very popular.

5 famous
BERLIN SPEECHES
that changed world history

---

471 J.F. KENNEDY
John-F-Kennedy-Platz
Schöneberg ⑦
June 26, 1963

"Freedom is indivisible, and when one man is enslaved, all are not free. When all are free, then we can look forward to that day when this city will be joined as one, and this country, and this great Continent of Europe, in a peaceful and hopeful globe. (...) All free men, wherever they may live, are citizens of Berlin (...)"

472 MARTIN LUTHER KING
Waldbühne
September 13, 1964

"For just as we are proving to be the testing ground of races living together in spite of their differences, you are testing the possibility of co-existence for the two ideologies which now compete for world dominance. If ever there were a people who should be constantly sensitive to their destiny, the people of Berlin, East and West, should be they."

473 BRUCE SPRINGSTEEN

Concert in Weissensee
July 19, 1988

The Freie Deutsche Jugend (FDJ), The Communist Party's youth arm, had invited Springsteen as part of their strategy to calm down the country's increasingly restless youth. 300.000 East Germans attended the concert. Springsteen said: "I'm not here for any government. I've come to play rock'n'roll for you in the hope that one day all the barriers will be torn down." 16 months later, the Wall came down.

474 KLAUS WOWEREIT

Former Mayor
of Berlin in
a television interview
2004

"Berlin ist arm, aber sexy." ("Berlin is poor, but sexy.") The former (gay) mayor of Berlin said this in an attempt to attract creative types to the city and it worked. Berlin's cheap rents and sparkling cultural life contributed to the effervescent start-up scene (think of Soundcloud or Zalando for example). According to *The Local* a new start-up is founded every 20 minutes in Berlin and the industry is set to produce thousands of new jobs in the coming years.

475 RONALD REAGAN

Brandenburg gate
in front of the Wall
June 12, 1987

"There is one sign the Soviets can make that would be unmistakable, that would advance dramatically the cause of freedom and peace. General Secretary Gorbachev, if you seek peace, if you seek prosperity for the Soviet Union and Eastern Europe, if you seek liberalization: Come here to this gate! Mr. Gorbachev, open this gate! Mr. Gorbachev, tear down this Wall!"

5

B O O K S

in which Berlin plays a main role

476 **BERLIN, IMAGINE A CITY**
RORY MACLEAN, 2014
rorymaclean.com/ books/berlin

This book should be read as a memoir, a history book and a fictional story at the same time. Travel writer Rory MacLean first visited Berlin in 1978 when he worked on the movie *Just a Gigolo* with David Bowie and Marlene Dietrich. He immediately fell in love with the city. The book assembles an eclectic cast of Berliners over five centuries.

477 **A WOMAN IN BERLIN**
ANONYMOUS, 2003

This is a diary of a 34-year-old journalist in Berlin starting on the 20th of April 1945, the day Berlin saw the face of war for the first time. The stunning account ends on the 22nd of June of that same year and the anonymous author describes her life in a city that's falling down and being sacked by the Russian army. The publication was very controversial in Germany because it reminded people of some uncomfortable truths.

478 GOODBYE TO BERLIN
CHRISTOPHER ISHERWOOD, 1939

Christopher Isherwood (1904-1986) was an Anglo-American writer who moved to Berlin in 1929, attracted by the exciting climate of the city in the Weimar-era and its limitless (sexual) possibilities for a gay writer. The musical *Cabaret* was based partly on *Goodbye to Berlin*.

479 FUNERAL IN BERLIN
LEN DEIGHTON, 1964

Funeral in Berlin is a perfect cold war spy mystery, a chronicle of the sixties in Berlin and a spellbinding tale of espionage. The basic premise is that the main character, a British spy, is in Berlin trying to arrange for the smuggling of a top Russian scientist from the East through the Berlin Wall back to the West.

480 WIR KINDER VOM BAHNHOF ZOO
CHRISTIANE F., 1978

This is the autobiography of Christiane F. (born Christiane Vera Felscherinow). It's the shocking story of a child prostitute and heroin addict living in West Berlin. The book was required reading in German schools for a long time, and producer Bernd Eichinger turned it into a film in 1981. The film featured Bowie's *Heroes* and was a huge success. It still serves as a warning for many.

5

TELEVISION SERIES

with scenes shot in Berlin

---

481 SENSE8
2015-2016

In this series, created by J. Michael Straczynski and the Wachowskis, eight strangers (Berlin actor Max Riemelt is one of them), living in different places around the world, find themselves linked together without knowing why. Slowly they discover they are 'sensates': otherwise normal humans who are mentally and emotionally connected. The scenes that take place in Berlin were shot on location and in the Babelsberg Studio.

482 DEUTSCHLAND 1983
2015

The German-American husband-and-wife team Anna and Jörg Winger created this mini-series (eight episodes) for the local broadcaster RTL. The story takes place in 1983, when Germany was in the centre of escalating nuclear brinkmanship between NATO and the Soviet Union. Parts of the show were filmed at the Stasi Museum.

483 BERLIN STATION
2016
berlinstation.com

This excellent show follows CIA agent Daniel Miller (Richard Armitage) who arrives at the CIA foreign station in Berlin. But the real star of this series is, without any doubt, the city of Berlin. Most of the scenes were shot on location in Berlin and Potsdam, and at Studio Babelberg in Potsdam.

484 TRANSLANTICS
2015

This web series is written and performed by digital artist Britta Thie. We're not sure if we should consider it a satire or deep soul searching, but she certainly has an interesting view on the often superficial Berliner start up and hipster scene – it's very recognizable. Shot in New York and in Berlin.

485 IM ANGESICHT DES VERBRECHENS (IN FACE OF THE CRIME)
2010

This highly acclaimed, multilayered and fast-paced TV series (ten episodes) unveils how things work in the Russian mafia scene in Berlin. It's about power shifts, the drama of human trafficking and the complexity of crime syndicates. Max Riemelt (who also stars in Sense8) plays one of the leading roles.

5 places with a very strong
DAVID BOWIE
signature

---

486 PARIS BAR

Kantstrasse 152
Charlottenburg ⑨
+49 (0)30 3138 052
parisbar.net

David Bowie lived in Berlin from 1976 to 1979 hoping to get rid of his cocaine-addiction. He and Iggy Pop liked to hang out in the stylish Paris Bar near Savignyplatz, which is still popular with artists and media-people. The notorious Rolling Stone interview that ended with Pop crawling out of the bar happened here.

487 HANSA STUDIOS

Köthener Strasse 38
Kreuzberg ②
+49 (0)30 2649 5330
hansastudios.de

This sound studio is where Bowie wrote the song *Heroes* and where he recorded three of his best albums; Low (1977), Heroes (1977) and Lodger (1979). It is said that Bowie later on in his career considered this trilogy to be his DNA. U2, Nick Cave, Depeche Mode, The Kooks, Travis... they all decided to work with Hansa. You can visit the cosy studios but don't forget to make a reservation.

488 HAUPTSTRASSE 155
Schöneberg ⑦

This is the apartment Bowie shared with Iggy Pop. Since Bowie's death in January 2016, many people have been petitioning to change the name of the Hauptstrasse (Main Street) into Bowiestrasse, which of course would make so much more sense. Fritz Music Tours (*musictours-berlin.com*) offers tours of the city that include a stop at Hansa Studios and the flat.

489 POTSDAMER PLATZ
Mitte ①

In the thirties Potsdamer Platz used to be Berlin's Piccadilly Circus. In the seventies it became an empty, heavily fortified patch of land between East and West, surrounded by GDR watchtowers. Now it's a shiny commercial centre with shops, cinemas and the flagship Sony Centre. Bowie referred to it in his 2013 comeback single *Where are we now?*

490 BRÜCKE MUSEUM
Bussardsteig 9
Dahlem
+49 (0)30 8312 029
bruecke-museum.de

Coco, Bowie's caring assistant at the time, took Bowie to this museum that was named after the group of German artists who called themselves 'Die Brücke' (The Bridge): Ernst Ludwig Kirchner, Fritz Bleyl, Erich Heckel and Karl Schmidt-Rottluff. Bowie loved these expressionists' rough strokes and their melancholic moods and he was deeply moved and triggered by the works.

5 essential
BERLIN SOUNDRACKS

---

491 **LOU REED**
BERLIN, 1973

Lou Reed's third solo-album was deeply inspired by the Berliner atmosphere in the seventies – by people living there like Isherwood and Marlène Dietrich, and by movies like *Nosferatu*. The concept-album is a rock opera about a doomed couple. In almost 50 minutes of music Reed deals with subjects like prostitution, suicide, drugs, depression and domestic violence. The atmosphere is miles away from the dance craze and escapism of the nineties after the Wall came down.

492 **DAVID BOWIE**
HEROES, 1977

The view from the control room of the Hansa Studio on two lovers kissing in front of the Wall would inspire Bowie to write the title track of his album Heroes – the second of the three albums of the so-called Berlin trilogy he wrote together with Brian Eno. Low was released a few months earlier, Lodger in 1979.

493 RAMMSTEIN

We often think of Berlin as the city of techno and this is partly true of course, but Berlin is so much more than electronic music. In 1994 six Ossies (East Germans) came together to found Rammstein, a unique metal band that flirts with death, bondage, fetishism and cannibalism. It is one of the very few German (singing) bands that have conquered the world.

494 SEEED
DICKES B, 2001

Seeed represents the Berlin music scene of the 2000s: multiculti, fun, and very urban. The band consists of eleven musicians who bring a mix of dancehall, reggae, dub-ska and hiphop. They often collaborate with international musicians like Cee-Lo. One of Seeed's biggest hits was *Dickes B*, an ode to the city of Berlin.

495 PAUL KALKBRENNER (WITH FRITZ KALKBRENNER AND SASCHA FUNKE)
BERLIN CALLING, 2008

This is the soundtrack of the 2008 movie *Berlin Calling* by Hannes Stöhr. The film is about a DJ who tours clubs around the globe with his manager and girlfriend. On the eve of his biggest album release he is admitted to a psychiatric clinic after overdosing. Paul Kalkbrenner played the main role and the movie depicts the Berliner techno scene (and the drug abuse associated with it) quite accurately.

5
ICONIC BERLINERS

496 ALEXANDER VON HUMBOLDT
1769 – 1859

Alexander von Humboldt was a Prussian geographer, naturalist and explorer, and the brother of the Prussian minister, philosopher and linguist Wilhelm von Humboldt. The Humboldt Forum on the Schlossplatz, a brand new and controversial museum not to be missed, was named after them and features a permanent exposition about the two brothers.

497 ANITA BERBER
1899 – 1928

This lady embodies everything Berlin stood for in the twenties and still stands for now: sexual liberation, creativity, freedom and drugs. She was the first nude dancer in the city and her performances broke many boundaries and her overt bi-sexuality and drug addiction made her a scandal in the eyes of the public. Otto Dix painted a beautiful portrait of her. Anita Berber died young of TB, helped along by syphilis and her addiction to drugs.

498 KÄTHE KOLLWITZ
1867 – 1945
Kollwitz Museum
Fasanenstrasse 21
Charlottenburg ⑨

The sculptor, painter and pacifist Käthe Kollwitz is best known for portraying the social problems of the poor. Kollwitz spent a large part of her life in a modest abode on the now gentrified square that is named after her. She lost a son in WWI and a grandson in WWII. An enlarged copy of her Pieta sculpture now adorns the Neue Wache.

499 MARLÈNE DIETRICH
BERLIN 1901 – PARIS 1992

Marlène Dietrich was an actress and singer who represents Germany's golden era as one of the world's great artistic and intellectual centres. When the Nazi dictatorship began in the 1930s, Dietrich and many other artists and intellectuals chose exile, and she never came back to her hometown.

500 SVEN MARQUARDT
BORN 3 FEBRUARY 1962

Marquardt is best known as the legendary and sometimes feared head bouncer of the techno temple Berghain. In his memoir *Die Nacht ist Leben* (The night is life), released in 2014, he writes about his life in the eighties in East Germany and compares it to the contemporary techno scene. Marquardt is also a skilled photographer and uses only analogic cameras and natural light.

INDEX

COLOPHON

EDITING *and* **COMPOSING** — Nathalie Dewalhens — nathaliedewalhens.com

GRAPHIC DESIGN — Joke Gossé and doublebill.design

PHOTOGRAPHY — Philipp Bögle — philippboegle.com

ADDITIONAL PHOTOGRAPHY — p. 24-25, 45, 61, 95, 164, 173, 182, 188, 214, 217, 229, 237, 243: Silvie Bonne

COVER IMAGE — Haus Schwarzenberg (secret 318) — Silvie Bonne

The addresses in this book have been selected after thorough independent research by the author, in collaboration with Luster Publishing. The selection is solely based on personal evaluation of the business by the author. Nothing in this book was published in exchange for payment or benefits of any kind.

D/2022/12.005/18

ISBN 978 94 6058 3087

NUR 512, 510

© 2016 Luster Publishing, Antwerp

Fifth edition, June 2022 — Fifth reprint, June 2022

lusterpublishing.com — THE500HIDDENSECRETS.COM

info@lusterpublishing.com

Printed in Italy by Printer Trento.

MIX
Paper | Supporting responsible forestry
FSC® C015829